The Jesuit Assassinations

The Writings of Ellacuría, Martín-Baró and Segundo Montes, with a Chronology of the Investigation

(November 11, 1989 - October 22, 1990)

**Instituto de Estudios Centroamericanos
and El Rescate**

Sheed & Ward

Sheed & Ward™ is a service of National Catholic Reporter Publishing
Company, Inc.

Library of Congress Cataloguing in Publication

ISBN: 1-55612-409-0

Published by: Sheed & Ward
                115 E. Armour Blvd. P.O. Box 419492
                Kansas City, MO 64141-6492

To order, call: (800) 333-7373

Contents

Part I
The Writings of Ellacuría, Martín-Baró and Segundo Montes . 1

Part II
A Chronology of the Investigation

Acknowledgements

Special thanks to Jorge Hérnandez who compiled and wrote the introduction. To the many people who assisted on all the last minute details for the completion of this book—including Sonia Baires, Ian Balsillie, Gemma Burgos, Marcos Lester, Jill Gluck de la Llata, Carol Jones, Don McClay, Cecilia Vásquez, Tom Ward and many others—thank you.

Thanks are also due to Chris Faber, for your willingness to translate so much in so little time, so well. And to Laura Kelly, for your invaluable help with the editing.

Most of all, our deep appreciation and admiration for the many courageous people in El Salvador who have risked their lives in pursuit of a just society.

List of Key Persons

Victims of the murders at the University of Central America, "José Simeon Cañas" (UCA), on November 16, 1989:

Father Ignacio Ellacuría, Rector
Father Martín Baró, Vice-Rector
Father Segundo Montes, Director of the Institute of Human Rights, IDHUCA
Father Amando López, Coordinator of Philosophy Department
Father Juan Ramon Moreno, Assistant Director of the Pastoral Center
Father Joaquin López y López, Director of "Fe y Alegria"
Elba Ramos, cook for the Jesuit House
Celia Marisela Ramos, 15, daughter of Elba Ramos

Those placed under arrest in January, 1990:

Col. Guillermo Alfredo Benavides Moreno, Director of the Military School "General Gerardo Barrios"
Lt. José Ricardo Espinosa Guerra, Company Commander of a commando unit of the Atlacatl Battalion
Lt. Yusshy René Mendoza Vallecillos, Section Commander, Military School 1st Lt.
Gonzalo Guevara Cerritos, Member of Commando Unit Atlacatl
Sgt. Antonio Ramiro Avalos Vargas, "Satanás," Member of Commando Unit Atlacatl
Sgt. Tomas Zapata Castillo, Member of Commando Unit Atlacatl
Cpl. Angel Pérez Vásquez, Member of Commando Unit Atlacatl
Pvt. Oscar Mariano Amaya Grimaldi, "Pilijay," Member of Commando Unit Atlacatl
Pvt. Jorge Alberto Sierra Ascencio (deserted in December), Member of Commando Unit Atlacatl

Officials of the Salvadoran Government:

Alfredo Cristiani, President of the Republic of El Salvador
Mauricio Eduardo Colorado, Attorney General (until May 1990)
Roberto Antonio Mendoza, Attorney General (beginning June 1990)
Roberto D'Aubuisson, Majority Leader of the Assembly
Mauricio Gutierrez Castro, Supreme Court President

Leaders of Armed Forces, November 16, 1989:

Gen. Rafael Humberto Larios López, Minister of Defense
Col. Juan Orlando Zépeda, Vice-Minister of Defense
Col. René Emilio Ponce Torres, Chief of Staff
Gen. Juan Rafael Bustillo, Commander of the Air Force
Col. Carlos Amando Avilés Buitrago, Chief of Psychological Operations
Col. Oscar Alberto León Linares, Commander of Atlacatl Battalion
Col. Hector Heriberto Hérnandez, Commander of the Treasury Police
Col. Francisco Elena Fuentes, Commander of the 1st Brigade
Col. Mauricio Ernesto Vargas, Commander of the 3rd Brigade

Director of the Special Investigations Unit:

Lt. Col. Manuel Antonio Rivas Mejia

Criminal Court Judge for the case, 4th District San Salvador:

Dr. Ricardo Zamora

United States Embassy Officials in San Salvador:

William Walker, Ambassador to El Salvador
Col. Milton Mejivar, Head of Military Group
Maj. Eric Buckland, Member of Military Group who received third-hand information implicating Col. Benavides in the murders.

Church Officials:

Msgr. Rivera y Damas, Archbishop of El Salvador
Msgr. Rosa Chávez, Auxiliary Bishop of El Salvador
Father José María Tojeira, Jesuit Provincial for Central America
Medardo Gomez, Lutheran Bishop of El Salvador
Father Miguel Francisco Estrada, Dean of Business Administration at the UCA, replaces Father Ellacuría as Rector of UCA

Additional Key People:

Lucia Barrera de Cerna, witness
Dr. María Julia Hérnandez, Director of the Archdiocese Human Rights Office, Tutela Legal
Abdulio Lozano López, husband of Elba Ramos, gardener at the UCA

Sources

Salvadoran Media Sources:

Carta A Las Iglesias An information service of the Pastoral Center of the University of El Salvador "José Simeon Cañas," UCA.

COPREFA: Press Office of the Armed Forces, Col. Mauricio de Jesus Chávez Caceres, Commander.

Diario de Hoy (DH) The most conservative newspaper in the country of El Salvador. Circulation 87,000.

Diario Latino (DL) An independent daily newspaper which has come under attack for its publications of the transcript of the April 22nd CBS "60 Minutes" report on the Jesuit case, the entire Moakley Special Committee Report, and the May 21st report by the Arms Control and Foreign Policy Caucus analysis of the Salvadoran High Command's human rights records. Circulation 49,000.

El Mundo (EM) An evening paper. Circulation 61,000.

La Prensa Grafica (LPG) A conservative paper that generally presents the government's perspective. Circulation 105,000.

National Network The goverment's official television transmission.

Proceso A liberal weekly publication of analysis and daily news on El Salvador, published by UCA.

TV 6 A private commercial channel that also has developed an "objective" attitude towards the news, based on the presentation of daily interviews with a variety of persons.

TV 12 Owned by members of the Christian Democrat party. Generally reports several perspectives (e.g., FMLN, the government, the U.S.). During the FMLN's November '89 offensive, the station momentarily shut down its transmissions in protest over government censorship.

Radio Horizonte A recently established commercial radio station.

Radio Sonora A mainstream commercial radio, has correspondents covering the news throughout the country.

Radio Venceremos (RV) A daily radio transmission of the Farabundo Marti National Liberation Front, FMLN.

Radio YSKL A mainstream commercial radio station.

Radio YSU The oldest commercial radio station in El Salvador; offers a mainstream perspective.

Other Media Sources:

Associated Press (AP) An international news wire service.

Los Angeles Times (LAT) Los Angeles' daily newspaper with national circulation.

Deutchland Press Agency (DPA) A German news wire service.

Miami Herald (MH) Miami's daily newspaper with national circulation.

New York Times (NYT) One of three leading United States newspapers with international circulation.

Uno Mas Uno A daily Mexican newspaper.

Washington Post (WP) One of three leading U.S. newspapers.

Cable News Network (CNN) International cable news network.

CBS "Sixty Minutes" Weekly national television documentary focusing on investigative reporting.

Reports:

Lawyers Committee The Lawyers Committee for Human Rights, a public interest law firm focusing on the issue of human rights; has issued a series of reports on the Jesuit assassinations and subsequent investigation.

Moakley Report The "Interim Report of the Speaker's Task Force on El Salvador," issued on April 30, 1990. Congressman Moakley is chairman of the Task Force.

U.S. Embassy Reports Reports issued by the United States Embassy in San Salvador.

Acronyms

AID	U.S. Agency for International Development
ANEP	Asociación Nacional de la Empresa Privada/National Association of Private Enterprise
ANTEL	National Telephone Company
ARENA	Alianza Republicana Nacionalista/Nationalist Republican Alliance
CEAT	Commando Especial Anti-Terrorista/Special Anti-Terrorist Command
CEBRI	Centro de Batallones de Reacción Inmediata/Center of Immediate Reaction Battalion
CEDES	Conferencia Episcopal de El Salvador/Salvadoran Bishops Conference
CEL	National Electric Company
CIA	U.S. Central Intelligence Agency
CITFA	Centro de Investigaciones y Transmisiones de la Fuerza Armada/Armed Forces Center for Investigations and Transmissions
COACES	Confederación de Asociaciones de Cooperativas de El Salvador/Confederation of Salvadoran Cooperative Associations
CODEHUCA	Comision de Derechos Humanos de Centroamerica/Central American Human Rights Commission
COPREFA	Comité de Prensa de la Fuerza Armada/Press Office of the Armed Forces
COT	Centro de Operaciones Tácticas/Center of Tactical Operations
CPDN	Comité Permanente del Debate Nacional/Permanent Committee of the National Debate
C3	Department of Operations of the High Command

C5	Department of Psychological Operations of the High Command
DIA	U.S. Defense Intelligence Agency
DM	Destacamento Militar/Military Detachment
DNI	Departamento Nacional de Inteligencia/National Intelligence Agency
"DT"	"Terrorista Delincuente"/Terrorist Delinquent
EM	Esquadrones de la Muerte/Death Squads
ESA	Ejército Secreto Anti-Communista/Secret Anti-Communist Army
FBI	U.S. Federal Bureau of Investigations
FENASTRAS	Federación Nacional Sindical de Trabajadores Salvadoreños/National Trade Union Federation of Salvadoran Workers
FMLN	Frente Farabundo Marti Para la Liberación Nacional/Farabundo Marti National Liberation Front
GAS	Gremio Anti-Communista Salvadoreño/ Salvadoran Anti-Communist Guild
IDHUCA	Instituto de Derechos Humanos de la Universidad Centroamericana/University of Central America Human Rights Institute
MAC	Movimiento Autentico Cristiano/Authentic Christian Movement
MILGROUP	U.S. Military Group
PADECOES	Patronato para el Desarrollo y Cooperación de El Salvador/Council for the Development and Cooperation of El Salvador
PDC	Partido Democrata Cristiano/Christian Democrat Party
SIC	Sección de Investigaciónes Criminales/Criminal Investigation Section
SIU	Special Investigations Unit

UGB	Union Guerrera Blanca/White Warriors Union
UCA	Universidad Centroamericana "José Simeon Cañas"/University of Central America "Jose Simeon Canas"
UDN	Union Democratica Nacionalista/Nationalist Democratic Union
UNTS	Union Nacional de los Trabajadores Salvadoreños/National Union of Salvadoran Workers

Foreword

On November 16, 1989, in the middle of the night, six of the most respected Jesuit priests in El Salvador, along with their housekeeper and her daughter, were brutally murdered by members of the Salvadoran military. Those who pulled the trigger and committed this heinous crime included men trained by American servicemen, on American soil, with American money. We all must bear some responsibility for this crime—in much the same way we must bear some responsibility for the war which has claimed over 70,000 lives.

On December 5th, Speaker of the House Tom Foley appointed me chairman of a nineteen member Special Task Force to monitor the Salvadoran government's investigation into the murders of the Jesuits and to report directly to him and the Congress. On April 30, 1990 we issued our first preliminary report. First among our general findings was that:

> The murders of the Jesuits reflect problems within the Salvadoran armed forces that go far beyond the actions of a particular unit on a particular night. Major reforms within the military are necessary to make a recurrence of such crimes unlikely; to insulate the judicial process from military pressure; and to strengthen Salvadoran democracy.

In our fact finding mission, my colleagues and I were dismayed by the military's continued blatant disregard for human life. As we stated in our report:

> Task Force members heard the murders of the Jesuits described by high military officials as 'stupid,' 'self-defeating,' and 'dumb.' But no military official with whom we talked said it was wrong.

Over the past decade, U.S. government policy has been based on the use of "test cases" as a measure of the progress of justice in El Salvador.

The murder of Archbishop Romero, 4 U.S. churchwomen, 74 indigenous people at Las Hojas, and 10 people at San Sebastián in 1988, among others, have been presented by various U.S. (embassy and administration) officials as 'test cases' of the Salvadoran judicial system. And as each 'test case' stalls because of death threats to prosecutors or the killing of judges and witnesses, a new atrocity is committed to fill the need for a new 'test case,' enabling the stalling to go on forever.

There is a danger that the smallest measure of justice in the case of the UCA murders will be presented by some as sufficient evidence that justice has at last come to El Salvador. This would be a serious injustice to the tens of thousands of Salvadoran people whose cases have received no attention, no outcry.

> *The institutional nature of the problem in El Salvador is demonstrated, as well, by the fact that the Jesuits' case reflects the Salvadoran justice system at its best, not its worst. This is one of a handful of the human rights cases in El Salvador over the past decade that has received enough international attention to be taken seriously by Salvadoran authorities. Thousands of other crimes, some perpetrated by the FMLN, some by the military, some by forces unknown, have not even been investigated. Despite a decade of promises, tens of millions of dollars in U.S. aid and repeated statements that progress is just around the corner, the Salvadoran justice system remains essentially an oxymoron— neither systematic, nor just.* [Task Force Report]

The following report by the El Rescate Human Rights Department and the Institute for Central American Studies provides invaluable information concerning the developments in the investigation of the UCA murders as well as a glimpse of the writings and works of the Jesuits. The 6 priests who were killed were leading intellectual and political thinkers of El Salvador. Indeed, they were seen as threats precisely because of their ability to reflect on the causes of the war. Their analysis provides an important legacy to understanding how to bring about a peaceful, negotiated solution to the war.

—Joseph Moakley
U.S. House of Representatives

"We do not want revenge, but we demand justice."
—Father José María Tojeira, Provincial
Jesuit Priest for Central America[1]

Introduction

When the idea first arose to write an homage to the Jesuit Fathers assassinated in El Salvador we planned to write an interpretive introduction to use with the chronology provided by the El Rescate Human Rights Department.[2] We felt that such a tribute would place this chronology into the global context of this heroic and tragic period of the history of El Salvador. However, we soon decided that the cold, appalling facts are sufficiently eloquent and need no additional comments.

And so we investigated the subject from another perspective. The chronology refers principally to the facts that pertain to the *deaths* of the Jesuits. We seek to emphasize their *lives*—and the way they viewed life—in the most difficult, yet most dignified moments of our history. We concluded that the only possibility of real value was to reflect on the themes of our national reality as found in the writings which constitute the legacy of the Jesuit Fathers.

We read the works of three of the martyrs: Ignacio Ellacuría, Ignacio Martín-Baró, and Segundo Montes, and we present their message here.

Thus it is not we who speak but they. And the most authentic demonstration that they lived what they preached was their physical deaths. They now live eternally in our consciousness. A repopulated town has already been named Segundo Montes, and a settlement named Ignacio Martín-Baró. Many Ignacios and Segundos will arise in the new generations of Salvadorans, as a heartfelt popular homage, because: "The poor of El Salvador cry for their dead, but more than anything else, they want what they died for to continue alive."[3]

The Salvadoran government and the United States government now talk of investigating the case of the six Jesuits.

We hope they do.

But isn't it much more important for the country to remember what they did in life?[4]

—Instituto de Estudios Centroamericanos

Part I

The Writings of Ellacuría, Martín-Baró, and Segundo Montes

Life teaches us that we must judge people by more than their words— i.e, by their actions, and, better yet, by the consistency between their theory and their practice. The work of the Jesuits in El Salvador is not an isolated event, but a commitment that they took upon themselves on a daily basis to accompany the people. Opening eyes and consciences. Seeking and finding roads toward a better life for the dispossessed. For that very reason their deaths were nothing new, since they were not the first.

This is how the Jesuits write those pages of history: "The profound changes that have occurred in the consciences of the majority of El Salvador's poor since the 1970s have always been viewed by the military and the powerful families of the oligarchy as the responsibility of priests' activities. They have always blamed the Church for opening the eyes of the oppressed so they could realize that they were oppressed and struggle not to be. That's why in 1977 they shouted 'Be a patriot, kill a priest!' and filled the country with pamphlets encouraging the murder of the religious. Perhaps in no other place in Latin America has the Theology of Liberation been made of so much flesh and blood, so alive, effective, mature and persistently transforming, as in El Salvador."

The history of these years is full of examples. The conversion and martyrdom of Monseñor Romero is the supreme example of a theology come alive, which fits in no book. In addition to the Archbishop, and these six brothers taken from us, 18 other priests have been assassinated to date. In the name of "anti-communism," they have been murdered by a "western and Christian democracy."

The first priest assassinated was a Salvadoran Jesuit, Father Rutilio Grande, who was ambushed and machine-gunned to death on a road on March 12, 1977 by government gunmen. All those recently assassinated in the Central American University knew "Tilo" (Rutilio Grande), the first martyr, and learned from him in the years when change was maturing, paths for organizing were opened up, and the poor were beginning their struggle to cease being poor.

Rutilio Grande began work in the rural areas in 1972, in the parish of Aguilares. This "pastoral experience" would distinguish the work of the Jesuits of Central America.

"From 1972 to 1977, Father Rutilio Grande and the team of Jesuits from Aguilares were transforming that extensive peasant region into a space for organization, Christian commitment, and community consciousness. During all these years, the relationships that united the Aguilares team with the team from the Central American University in San Salvador were close, above all through the generation of young Jesuits who learned to work pastorally with Rutilio Grande and to reflect intellectually with Ignacio Ellacuría. Both dedicated a good part of their time to teach the Jesuits who would later replace them. They complemented each other. Rutilio insisted that their pastoral work should be enlightened by analyses done with maximum theoretical rigor. Ellacuría insisted on a theoretical reflection which was always being born from direct action."[5]

They had many successes in their social practice, and made many errors, but they were not mistaken in defining their own role in Salvadoran society and they took it on with a historical responsibility and a singular courage. This is how they viewed their role in their country: "As a social scientist it isn't easy living within a process so convulsive. It isn't easy for many reasons, some intrinsic, others extrinsic. The most obvious difficulty comes from the risk to the lives of those who try to shed light on the root problems of the conflict or contribute to the search for their solution. It is easier to ignore reality when that reality is so expressive, so clear as to its meaning, that the simple act of speaking of it with truth constitutes a "subversive" act. If calling reality by its true name transformed Monseñor Romero into a prophet for his people, into the voice of those without voice, it also transformed him into a revolutionary and a subversive for the established powers that be. Three days after his moving call to the police forces 'In the name of God, stop the repression!' he was assassinated while celebrating the Eucharist."[6]

The Central American University, "José Simeon Cañas," was Ellacuría's life project, the fundamental realization of his work which, because of its social commitment, was soon transformed into a target of the oppressors. Ellacuría viewed the role of the University as complex.

"The point of departure for our conception of what a University should be was affected by two considerations. The first, and most obvious, has to do with culture, with knowledge, with a determined exercise of the rational intellect. The second, these days not so obvious or common, is that the University is a social reality and a social force, historically marked by what the society in which it functions is, and which it is destined to enlighten and transform, as a social force that is both the reality in which it lives, and for which it must live. . . .

"Our intellectual analysis is that our historical reality, the reality of El Salvador, the reality of the Third World, that is, the reality of the larger part of the world and the historical reality that is most universal, is characterized fundamentally by the effective predominance of falsehood over truth, of injustice over justice, of oppression over liberty, of scarcity over abundance, in short, of evil over good. . . .

"Immersed in that reality, possessed by it, we ask ourselves what to do with the University. And we answer, above all, from the ethical point of view: transform it, do what is possible so that good wins over evil, liberty over oppression, justice over injustice, truth over falsehood and love over hate. We cannot understand the validity of a University, and less still one inspired by Christian faith, without this commitment and without this decision. . . . A university inspired by Christian faith is one which focuses all of its university activities . . . from the illuminating perspective of what a preferential option for the poor means . . . The University should make itself felt among the intellectually poor, in order to be a science for those who have no science, an elucidating voice for those without voice, an intellectual support for those, who in their own reality, have truth and reason, though at times in a dispossessed way, but who do not have the academic rationality to justify and legitimize their truth and their reason. . . .

"Our University has modestly tried to place itself on this difficult and confrontational line of action. It has obtained some results through its research, its publications, its denouncements; but most of all through a few men who have given up other, more brilliant, ordinary profitable professions, in order to give themselves vocationally to the universal liberation of the Salvadoran people; in some cases through students and professors who have paid painfully with their own lives, with exile, with ostracism, for their contribution to the university service for the oppressed majority. . . . For this work we have been brutally persecuted. . . . If our

University had not suffered during these years of passion and death for the Salvadoran people, it would not have been fulfilling its mission as a University, and less still would it have been demonstrating its Christian inspiration. In a world where falsehoods, injustice and repression rule, a university which struggles for truth, for justice and for liberty cannot expect less than to be persecuted."[7]

Without viewing themselves as possessing the absolute truth, they defended their beliefs passionately. Martín-Baró wrote in the Prologue to one of his works, "It is also possible that some of the pages that follow lack antiseptic cleanliness, that seems to us to be an ideological deception, but therefore lacks that cold objectivity that is usually recommended in the academic world. What remains as an explanation is the fact that many of them have been written in the heat of events, in the middle of a police surveillance on one's own home, after the assassination of a colleague or under the physical and moral impact of a bomb that has destroyed the office where one works. But we also believe, perhaps erroneously, that these experiences are what permit one to enter into the world of the oppressed, to feel, from a little closer, the experience of those who carry years of oppression on their (class) shoulders, and who today are emerging into a new history. There are truths that can only be discovered through suffering or from the critical vantage point of extreme situations."[8]

They analyzed the country's situation with the same courage and uncompromising stance. Ellacuría said at the beginning of 1981, "Since the end of 1976, with the failure of Colonel Arturo Armando Molina's attempt at Agrarian Reform, there is a steady increase of repressive actions and an accelerated polarization of the parties in the conflict. The regime had already begun to feel not only the unending urgency of the reforms but also the accelerated development of popular organizations. At that time, it was thought that a coup d'etat against the oligarchy, which is what the incipient expropriation of land was, could initiate a controlled reformism which would resolve the structural problems of the country and take the social base away from the popular movements."

"The defeat of the reformist project of 1976 accelerated and aggravated the process of repression by giving a free hand to the oligarchy's forces, which had seen themselves seriously threatened. In the beginning the repression struck democratic sectors that were thwarted in the elections of 1977 and repressed them until they were almost obliterated from the political scene."

In his analysis, Ellacuría stresses, "But everything began much earlier. The underlying reality of this extreme situation is not the repression, but the structural injustice and the institutionalized violence, which, based on an immoral distribution in the ownership of resources, has created an economic, social, political and military structure that is ultimately responsible and the originating cause of what is currently happening in El Salvador."[9]

He writes frankly, "We have a situation in which El Salvador suffers not only from an intolerable structural injustice, but also from a violent struggle between those who fundamentally defend the status quo and those who are against it. But the opposition is no longer purely ideological or economic. The struggle is not about who is going to end up being the economic power, but rather it is a political and military struggle about who will end up being the political power and the military power." He continues, "So structural reforms are not enough, rather it is necessary to determine who will ultimately defend those structural reforms, that is, who will have the political and military power.[10]

And he concludes, "There has been a relentless blocking of political solutions to El Salvador's problems. The electoral road was blocked in 1972 and in 1977. The road to reforms was blocked in 1973 and in 1976. The non-violent military coup d'etat and the 'Foro Popular' coalition of October 15, 1979 was blocked. The process of organization and mobilization of people that constituted a considerable force from 1975 to 1980 was blocked. The social force of the political parties was nullified. And this along with everything else had to do with the search for a political solution."[11]

But in no way are we dealing with mechanical conclusions which alienate human beings and their desires, since, "From this point of view, the proponents of a political-military solution should consider, above all, the objective necessities of our national reality and the just demands of the organized people. Objective necessities orient solutions toward answers acceptable to the majority of the people, no matter what their social position, while the just demands of the organized people indicate the minimums that should be reached so that they are not defrauded. It is they who, with so many sacrifices and with so many dead, have pushed forward a profound process of national renewal. It serves little to accuse them of being inspired by Marxism or of having Communism as their final goal. Both of these accusations are inexact, if not entirely false. And no one can deny that the organized people have been the principal actors in a process wherein they have been asking to live as all human beings, and men and women who work, deserve. Hence, the satisfaction of their just demands is an unavoidable condition, not only as a response to their rights, but to find the most adequate and correct solutions."

Fatalism is completely foreign to Ellacuría. He concludes that "El Salvador's historical circumstances have made military confrontation inevitable. What remains to be done now is to reduce it to rational forms and limits, conforming to the universally recognized rules of war. The civil war should be recognized by the international community, at least *de facto*. Political factors should also moderate strictly military factors here. And, of course, power alone cannot be permitted to represent the legality and rationality of the State, which uses and abuses force to ignore objective and legal demands, without which a government loses its reason for existence."[12]

In another of his works, he returns to the theme, " . . . the civil war which, since 1981, has scorched El Salvador, has sunk its roots in a history of centuries-old oppression, a true incubator of violence that today threatens the country. Therefore, a realistic analysis of the violence in El Salvador requires a historical review, since the continuing violation of the most fundamental human rights has produced an explosive accumulation of frustrated aspirations, of just demands repressed.

"In 1932, as a consequence of the grave world crisis, a popular rebellion, mostly of indigenous Salvadoran groups, was drowned in blood. Since then, the Salvadoran regime has maintained its structures of domination, relying on a rigid military or paramilitary control of the popular and union movements, while the reformist projects attempted by various government leaders have not altered the fundamental schemes of oppression. At the beginning of the 1970s, the outlines of a serious social conflict began to take shape, with the emergence of popular demands in a consistently more organized manner, and with the closing off, time and time again, of all solutions which disposed of the system. With the coup d'etat of 1979, the conflict entered an accelerated and more defined phase which unleashed a genuine civil war."[13]

Ignacio Martín-Baró's analysis also points to courses to follow without hiding the difficulties, "Very serious problems of all kinds created by the civil war in El Salvador do no more than place in sharp focus the unsustainable social base upon which an attempt is being made to build a coexistence for only a few people. To build new forms of social life, more just and dignified, constitutes a gigantic task. We will have to overcome not only the intransigence of the oligarchy, or the military obstinance of the Reaganites here and there, but also, the weaknesses and the fatigue of the popular sectors, which in certain moments feel tempted to look back through the windows of dependency or the alluring lull of submission."[14]

Martín-Baró extended his analysis to the situation in the rest of Central America, "The massive violations of human rights committed during these years in almost all the countries of the area have been material for ridicule in the civilized world. The brutality of the Somoza regime toward the civilian population is well known, matched only by its insatiable greed for wealth. One and the other precipitated their fall in the face of multi-class forces, united behind the flag of Sandino. But neighboring regimes have not taken a back seat in acts of brutality and have even surpassed them in cruelty. The tremendous massacres of indigenous peoples in Guatemala or of rural workers in El Salvador, the continuing recourse to the 'disappearance' of workers and professionals, the assassination of more than twenty priests, including the Archbishop, the widespread appearance of decapitated bodies and bodies thrown into public waste bins, are some of the colder examples of a repressive wave that has made the Central American regimes cheerful emulators of the doctrine of 'national security' practiced in South America. Forty thousand victims of political repression in a period of three years in a country like El Salvador, with a population that doesn't reach even five million inhabitants,[15] is testimony to a new "genocide" carried out in the name of anti-communism, which is only a camouflage for those interested in exploitation."[16]

Martín-Baró denounces, " . . . the violence of the political repression . . . quantitatively and qualitatively constitutes the trademark that has stigmatized El Salvador in the last few years, and which has transformed it into a central focus of criticism for all the institutions defending human rights. . . . The actors are the so-called security forces (that is, the police forces), combined forces of the army or simply military groups linked to the security forces or operating with their support and collusion.[17]

" . . . To understand the qualitative magnitude of the violence in El Salvador one must include the aspect of cruelty that saturates many of the acts of violence. Above all, there is the systematic practice of torture used against those who fall into the hands of the police. A cadaver that does not show evidence of rape and physical harm on the body, often deformed, is rare. But above all, there is the practice of cutting the body in pieces and exhibiting it in a macabre manner: cadavers that appear spread out in pieces by the sides of the roads or thrown in garbage cans, mothers with their bellies opened and the fetus cut out, heads without bodies hung from the branches of trees or on the wall of some building, bodies without heads exposed and with signs with the name of some 'death squad' written on them."[18]

The writings of the Jesuits, however, were not merely criticism of current conditions. Martín-Baró further analyzes the roots of the situation: "Salvadoran society, like other Latin American societies, finds itself deeply split in groups whose interests are irreconcilable. This irreconcilability of social interests is at the root of the objective opposition between two principal groups. . . . In every moment the existing social order is the product of the balance of social forces. Therefore, the social order maintained in El Salvador is the product of the domination of a small minority over the large populace . . . a state of dominating violence by the few against the many, of the powerful against the weak. This situation has been marked by structural violence and has been denounced as an 'established chaos.'"

"It does not take much analysis to demonstrate the structural violence in El Salvador. It is sufficient to cite some of the situations maintained by the system which block the majority from the possibility of satisfying their basic needs, even in the most elemental way. The distribution of resources earned is such that three out of every four Salvadoran children suffer, one of every two adult Salvadorans is illiterate and, on an average, a Salvadoran hardly has the possibility of access to medical attention once every two years."

However, he continues, "Structural violence cannot be reduced to an inadequate distribution of available resources which impede the satisfaction of the basic necessities of the majority. Structural violence also includes an ordering of that oppressive inequality, through the use of legislation which hides behind the mechanisms of the social distribution of wealth and establishes a coercive force obligating people to respect them. The system therefore closes the cycle of violence, justifying and protecting those structures that privilege the few at the cost of the many. Even more, control over social institutions permits the dominating class to impose its objectives over the entire society. . . . Since the social order is a product of, and reflects, the domination of one social class over the rest, the most important conclusion that follows from this is also the most obvious: violence is already present in the social order and, therefore, it is not arbitrary to speak of structural violence. This violence is not the violence perpetrated by individuals; nor is it necessary that a personal consciousness exist about it. On the contrary, we are dealing with the violence of the whole of society and, while it does not enter into a crisis, it is imposed with the unconscious naturalness of a reflex action. But that the violence is there and that a continued coercion is imposed on the oppressed classes has been shown to be true historically with the nonviolent civil disobedience movements. With their peaceful refusals to follow the rules of the game, the followers of Ghandi, Martin Luther King, Jr. and Monseñor Helder Camara aroused the violence of the system, which went into the streets to impose by military force those coercive demands that feed the privileges of the social sector in power."[19]

Analyzing the theme of violence more deeply, the writings of the Jesuit reveal, "Open violence as a possibility of human beings, used and developed through processes of socialization, finds its ultimate definition in its justification. . . . Every act of violence requires a social justification and, when this is lacking, generates one by itself. . . . It is a fact that every social order determines the forms and degrees of permissible violence . . . there are four elements which function to define what constitutes socially acceptable violence: who can carry it out, against whom, in what circumstances, and to what degree. . . . Now, since the social order is based not so much on a consensus of the entire population as on the domination achieved by one class, the fundamental factor justifying violence consists in defining how violence is beneficial for the interests of that social class. In the case where those interests are in danger, the four elements can be ignored and in fact they are . . . Now, the same class character of the social order and of the justified violence influences its possible rejection by those who have different or opposing social interests. The violence justified in function of some partial interests becomes an unacceptable violence for those who do not participate in those interests and even more for those who become victims of that violence for maintaining interests foreign to them."

"The social definition of violence is definitely a powerful weapon employed by the dominating class from a position of power. The character of the violence and the aggression is not determined so much by the act itself as by its effect. This is what has happened in the last few years with respect to the definition of terrorism. In principle, terrorism is defined by the dictionary as 'domination by terror, that succession of acts of violence executed to instill terror.'"[20]

" . . . Nevertheless, an objective analysis that tries to examine the facts in light of the definition, will find that terrorism is one of the strategies most often used by dictatorships and tyrannies to conserve their power."[21]

"The war in El Salvador is even more enlightening. For the social communications media, the only terrorists are the insurgent groups and their actions. Nevertheless, the acts of terror are carried out, almost without exception, by government or paramilitary forces linked to the economic and political powers in the country. While the official version labels as terrorism sabotage against the energy or communication systems carried out by the insurgent forces, it is silent on, or even justifies as acts of patriotic heroism, the continuing chain of searches, kidnappings, campaigns encouraging [accusations], 'disappearances' of persons, systematic torture, harassment of private lives, bombings, assassinations, macabre exhibitionism and collective massacres. These events are what fundamentally keep the Salvadoran population terrorized and have prevented the insurgency from taking over the reins of political power in the country."[22]

Emphasizing the historical character of violence, Martín-Baró considers it impossible to understand it outside of the social context in which it develops. "One of the most fallacious points of view is the condemnation of violence 'from wherever it may come,' which disregards its origin, meaning and effect. It isn't surprising that this sort of viewpoint comes from social groups who attempt to place themselves above conflicts, although they find themselves linked to the forces in power. The soldier killed in a confrontation with insurgent forces is one thing. The unionist taken from his house, tortured and assassinated by police forces tied to the regime is something very different. The occupation of a public building or factory by force to make just labor demands is one thing. To attack strikers or protesters with bombs and automatic rifles is something else."[23]

According to Segundo Montes, an examination of the national reality makes the theme of human rights obligatory. "Human rights in El Salvador have become an object of study, observation and repeated condemnation in the present decade. When speaking of the violation of human rights in this country, explicit reference is made to civil and political rights that are trampled on. Not without reason, since the violence, the repression and the war have caused the deaths of more than 60,000 people, thousands of captured, and perhaps more than 3,000 forced disappearances during this period. All this without the judicial system being able to touch the problem by even condemning the authors, much less effectively bringing a percentage of the cases to the courts in an effort to force new behaviors and make the restoration of some real norms of minimally acceptable social coexistence possible. The urgent necessity to save human lives, to stop the violation of the more obvious and prevailing human rights, can make one forget or lose the structural perspective that underlies so many violations, and which has been and continues to be the cause for the social pressure for changes. That pressure is inhibited or repressed violently."

In his treatment of the theme of human rights, Segundo Montes "tries to analyze the structural core of systematic human rights violations, which includes the combination of economic, social and cultural rights, which makes material, social, and spiritual reproduction impossible for the immense majority of Salvadorans. It is true that the years of the current decade have deteriorated the living conditions of the population, because of the war and the integral crisis of the society. But the figures for the years before the development of the crisis are sufficiently eloquent, to understand both the consistent emergence of unions and popular organizations and revolutionary organizations, as well as the two-fold combination of reform and repression which was used in an attempt to avoid radical change . . . beginning with the coup d'etat of October 15, 1979, which introduced the worst violation of civil and political rights in El Salvador's history."[24]

The Jesuits warn of "explanations" which divert attention from the true causes of the problem. "The deterioration caused by the civil war and the crisis the country is experiencing can be blamed, not without reason, for the deterioration in the living standards of the poor majority, because of the impossibility of directing sufficient funds to fulfill the commitments pledged in the Constitution and in international agreements, covenants and treaties, with respect to economic, social and cultural rights. But by no means can that be considered the root of the problem. In official statistics that support this idea, it is clear that a structural situation obstructing the satisfaction of the needs and the above-stated rights for a disproportionate majority of the population existed before the crisis began. Even more, during the entire previous decade those structures became markedly and progressively inequitable to the advantage of a small minority, and with this unequal distribution by social strata, life for the majority became impossible. The data demonstrates a structural situation of permanent, systematic and progressive violation of the economic, social and cultural rights of the majority, as much as can be measured by the statistics and the figures presented."[25]

"Two legitimate means exist to obtain income figures: work and the ownership of the means of production. With respect to the former, we have already seen that the possibilities for work are insufficient to meet the demand of the working age population and hence the possibilities of finding work are few. With respect to the latter, the category of 'micro businesses' encompasses 74.9% of all the 'private Salvadoran businesses,' and 98% of all businesses if we add 'small businesses' to it. The majority of 'micro businesses' bring in at most a subsistence salary to its proprietors. On the average, 'small businesses' do not generate more that one paid job for every three businesses. In these 'businesses' one finds 7.8 percent of the known PEA [workforce] in El Salvador."[26]

"It is important to stress . . . that the predominant wealth of the country lies in agriculture and livestock production, that the strongest sector of the economy is agriculture, that the major source of foreign exchange from exports comes from agricultural products, and yet there is an insufficient amount of food for the population. A productive and economic structure of this nature is, by itself, inequitable and therefore a violation of the obligation to provide to the inhabitants the minimum demand for the nationally and internationally recognized right to food."[27]

Noting that the infant mortality (of those less than one-year-old with respect to live births) is a clear indicator of the living conditions of the population, Segundo Montes writes: "In consequence, and taking into account the rate of live births, the number of children less than one-year-old that have died in El Salvador in the contemplated period is approximately . . . greater than 14,000 per year over the last decade and greater than 10,000 per year in the present decade. That difference is due not only to the improvement of living conditions, but also to a supposed diminution of births."[28]

"The causes of mortality, both infant and maternal, would be eliminated for the most part with some nutritional, hygenic and health conditions that today are generally accessible to persons if they have at their disposal the minimum economic resources of a modern society."[29]

"The preceding sections have demonstrated at length, category by category, how the systems and structures in force in the country do not allow for even the minimally necessary living conditions for the majority in this country today, and is thus in violation of economic, social, cultural and human rights for the greater part of the population. The State, as a signatory to and as the guarantor of the juridical and contractual obligations of international conventions and internal legislation, has not implemented the measures required for their fulfillment."[30]

"Socioeconomic analysis offers us a contrast between the ideals and obligations formulated in the Constitution and in other juridical standards, and the reality established by empirical data and indicators. If one analyzes the legislation, one cannot help but admire both the principles that sustain the Political Constitution from its first article, as well as the standards and obligations expressed in the rest of the articles relative to such rights, and the promises that contract the State and the society in implementing them. On the other hand, for the majority of the population, the empirical data regarding those principles and rights apparently reveal a society distinct from that which the Constitution and national and international legislation aspire. It appears more likely—given the assumption that both aspects refer to the same society—that there exists in El Salvador a permanent state of anticonstitutionality. Or, seen from the opposite perspective, it would seem that the Constitution, the international commitments and the rest of the normative and obligative legislation in this matter refer to some society distinct from Salvadoran society.

"While the human being is recognized as the origin and the end purpose of the activity of the State (Art. 1, Political Constitution of 1983), that 'human being' is not recognized either as human, nor as a being, in the reality reflected by the socioeconomic data, as published by official organizations. While, 'consequently, it is a State obligation to secure for the inhabitant of the Republic, the enjoyment of liberty, health, culture, economic well-being and social justice' (Art. 1, paragraph 2), that obligation has not been carried out or realized through effective practice for the majority of citizens. Not even a consistent and progressive process toward the fulfillment of such obligations can be perceived."[31]

"Life is the primary, basic and supreme good of the human individual; however the data show that although life is abundant in El Salvador, very soon it begins to be frustrated, by . . . living conditions which are difficult to consider as 'human' in accord with the acceptable minimum in today's civilized societies, or in accord with the legally formulated principles and obligations. Worse still, as a consequence of the above, for the majority of the population the prevalent characteristic of existence is a life which withers away from its inception, culminating in premature death."[32]

"The data show that rather than worsening, the standard of living has improved a little in the present decade—a function of urban construction and the migrations toward population centers—although it remains far from achieving acceptable levels."[33] Therefore, one cannot blame this problem on the crisis and the war . . . Just as the civil war produces death and destruction, so does poverty, unemployment, illness, lack of living, and minimal resources—and to an even greater extent."[34]

"It could be categorized not only as a permanent anti-constitutional situation, but as a systematic and structural violation or an intrinsically violating structure and system, including human rights, economic, social and cultural violations of the great majority. Any solution to the present crisis and the war has to include at least the modification of these structures and the systematic adaptation of these conditions, not only to respond to the obligation to the State and society but also to resolve the root causes of the conflict. The war could have a military finish, but if the structural problems which are at the base of injustice are not resolved, peace will not be achieved."[35]

The compression of the situation in the country carried with it the elaboration of the proposals for a solution. They were always fervent supporters of political-negotiated solutions, although their thinking was profoundly realistic: "One has to look at where we have come from and where we are going: the extreme right, here in the capital, in the army and the party, has maintained until only a short while ago that dialogue was antipatriotic. In this sense, to speak of dialogue is a great advance. There is a semantic and an emotional problem here. The right cannot accept the guerrilla theory of 'double power.' Therefore, they refuse to modify the Constitution and allow the participation of the FMLN in power and in the army, even though the FMLN has already given up at least these last two conditions."[36]

Returning to the international situation and its affect on the region and the country, Ellacuría writes in early 1989: ". . . the recent historical process of Central America, especially in Nicaragua and El Salvador, has to be seen as fundamentally determined by the conflict between the revolutionary Marxist movement and the dominant conservative capitalist movement. . . . This conflict of known characteristics in years past has entered a crisis and opens up another type, fundamentally new and superior. . ."[37]

Referring to the national opening, in an interview in September, he indicated: "My opinion is that we have entered into a new phase of the Salvadoran process. the most recalcitrant right feels betrayed by the Tela Accords. Minister of Defense Larios has declared that there can be dialogue but not negotiations. Cristiani, in the end, had achieved a consensus when, on June 11, he proposed an uninterrupted dialogue without conditions, by a commission. The PDC [Christian Democratic Party] and the Democratic Convergence, deciding not to give the trump card to Cristiani, made a mistake by not entering this commission which could not be considered extreme right. They would have been able to leave the commission later if it did not work. Cristiani was planning a serious process of dialogue that would have opened a breach in his party and he again offered to return to the Tela Accords without the previous condition of a cease-fire first."[38]

Starting from this problematic situation he concludes: "The revolutionary ends cannot be achieved at the moment by classic revolutionary means, but must be procured more slowly and through much work by new means, less violent, and with more liberty and pluralism."[39]

Earlier he noted that: "In the FMLN, more clearly than in any other primary sector, is reflected the dawn of a new phase, already a new beginning to the strategic project is being attempted, a change in attitude and tactics that . . . do not mean a departure with the essentials of their proposals, but a fundamental change in response to a fundamentally new situation." Nevertheless, "even with this change, the fundamental position of the FMLN . . . continues to be that its primary force is the united armed struggle for the popular insurrection and that the accompanying negotiation would have to insure their participation in government before going into elections, as well as the formation of only one army made up of the two which exist now. This means that the change, if in fact there is one, should not be seen as the concession of defeat. This defeat cannot be shown by any convincing means using the facts. But subjectively speaking, based or not on objective reasons, the conviction of the FMLN is completely distinct: they have never been as militarily and politically strong nor had better relations with the people as they have now and they can even improve in a very short time. There are no signs in these months of reflection to think that the FMLN doubts its military and insur-rectional power. Therefore, one cannot conclude that this change comes from a supposed weakness. The point of departure of their analysis and of their conciliatory move toward important concessions has not been, and is not, the abandonment by depletion of the principal element of their strategy but, at most, the persuasion of the difficulty of a military triumph as much in the short term as in terms of the social and economic costs for the country."

Ellacuría considers it necessary to point out that, "In spite of this prin-ciple and this logic, the FMLN had already reached the conclusion that El Salvador would not tolerate at the present time a Marxist-Leninist government." In a work cited previously, he expresses the political think-ing of the FMLN, that . . . "The possible and desirable revolution in El Salvador is not a Stalinist or Vietnamese revolution, as perhaps some thought earlier, but a democratic revolution which accepts pluralism of parties in elections, the open expression of the ideas and practices of the Western world, especially freedom of religion and the idiosyncracies and traditions of the Salvadoran people, the acceptance of a mixed economy which is open to private business and private property, and, of course, the freedom of expression and organization, and the maintenance of good relations with all countries, especially the United States."[40]

In an interview published two months before his death, to the question, "Do you consider that there is no future for an insurrectional revolt?" he responded, "for a long time we defended this thesis. Perhaps it is the point of greatest disagreement with the FMLN, but time has shown it to be so. In 1982, the sabotage of electricity or the declaration of a traffic stoppage inspired people to rise up. Today, to the contrary, it alienates much of the population, as has been shown in our opinion polls. Moreover, . . . [their strategy was] outlined last year by the General Command of the FMLN in what they called their Vatican II. From there emerged the proposal to participate in January elections. Still this process of 'dawning' is not ending and there are tactical vacillations, but if the climate in the country improves, the political struggle could replace the armed struggle."[41]

Greater pressure for dialogue is considered necessary: "In order to get the parties in the conflict to sit down to negotiate sincerely and effectively to help all the Salvadoran people and not only some sectors, there should be immense national pressure, made by all the political parties and all the social forces. The new opposition should fight primarily for this objective, the participants in the national debate should do so also, as should the Church, as a principal part of its mission, face the task with all its spiritual resources and its summoning power. The Church has already done something, but much more can be done. The old idea of a national referendum reflecting the people's will should be put in place."[42]

In early November, Ellacuría received the Alfonso Comín prize in Barcelona, in the name of the people of El Salvador. But the events beginning the night of the 11th did not detain his return to El Salvador.

"A few hours after the offensive began, the government transferred all the broadcasting stations to the army's station, Radio Cuzcatlán, in order to control all the information which was released. Calls from ARENA sympathizers which encouraged the elimination of the 'guilty parties' of this disorder were received at the station. On the list of those marked appeared one more time, 'Ignacio Ellacuría and the Jesuits of UCA.' The callers asked for their death. They also asked for the death of Archbishop Rivera y Damas and Bishop Rosa Chávez, the death of leaders of the UNTS labor union, the death of Ungo and Zamora, and leaders of the

Democratic Convergence. They asked for these deaths in the climate of
hate which the military radio station openly broadcast until, on the night
of the 15th, the assassination of the six priests was carried out.

"The violent waters constantly threatened the UCA. On July 22, a
group of soldiers placed four bombs which destroyed part of the university printing press. But there were not only dynamite attacks. There was
a worsening of the verbal campaign of ARENA and army spokespersons
against the Jesuits of the university, including, among many others, the
accusation that they were inspired by a 'pagan cardinal who celebrates
black masses to pagan gods' (Cardinal Arns of Brazil)."

In the second edition of July 1989, the biweekly publication of UCA,
"Letter to the Churches," judged that the official campaign of harassment
and violence against UCA was based on "fear of the truth."

"The principal reason is that UCA often becomes an objective adversary to the economic, political, and military projects of the government.
And it can be a powerful adversary, not because it has economic, political
or military power, but because it has a social power based on the University word which is rational and Christian. And if this word is the word of
truth, it becomes an uncomfortable power."

"Through its investigations and publications, UCA tries to reveal the
Salvadoran reality, analyze the causes of the current tragedy, and propose
the most humane and viable solutions. It exposes the truth, quantifying
and analyzing it: the human rights violations and those responsible, the
conditions of poverty and its causes, the number of refugees and its roots,
the events of the war and its impasse. UCA seeks to speak and analyze
the truth. This is what does not please and is intolerable for some."[43]

Amidst this daily struggle which he shared with his people, came the
16th of November: "Why don't you leave here, Father?   It is
dangerous . . ." "Because we have much to do, there is much work . . ."

The work to which Martín-Baró referred remained unfinished. That
morning, the armed forces entered through the Mons. Romero Pastoral
Center, next to the house of the priests, whose lives were cut short by a
waste of bullets. They also placed an accurate shot through the heart of a
photograph of Mons. Romero. "They know he still lives and they still
want to kill him!"[44]

To conclude, we join with the thought of another member of the Jesuit community of El Salvador, who survived only because he was outside the country: "These martyrs do not want revenge, nor are they interested that justice be brought about for them. What they want is peace and justice for El Salvador through the best means left to achieve them."[45]

Notes

1. Cited by Archbishop Arturo Rivera y Damas in his November 19th Homily in *La Basilica del Sagrado Corazon, San Salvador.*

2. El Rescate Human Rights Department, "A Chronology of the Jesuit Assassinations: The Investigation and Related Events: November 11, 1989 - October 22, 1990," mimeo, s.l., s.f.

3. Jon Sobrino, "Sobre el asesinato de los Jesuitas salvadoreños y su concepción de la Universidad," Estudios Sociales Centroamericanos, Vol. I, No. 52, January - April 1990, pp. 25.

4. Jon Sobrino, "Sobre el asesinato de los Jesuitas salvadoreños y su concepción de la Universidad," Estudios Sociales Centroamericanos, Vol. I, No. 52 January - April 1990, pp. 25.

5. Revista Envio Instituto Historico CA, AO 8, No.100, December 1989, pp. 4-5.

6. Ignacio Martín-Baró, "Acción e ideologia-psicologia social desde Centroamerica," Segundo Edición, San Salvador, UCA Editores, 1981, Prologo, pp. VII-VIII.

7. Ignacio Ellacuría, Graduation acceptance speech of Dr. Honoris Causa given at the University of Santa Clara, California, USA, in 1982. Cited by Jon Sobrino in "Sobre el asesinato de los Jesuitas salvadoreños y su concepción de la Universidad."

8. Ignacio Martín-Baró, "Acción e ideologia-psicologia social desde CA," Segunda Edición, San Salvador, UCA Editoras, 1985, Prologo, pp. IX-X.

9. Ignacio Ellacuría, "Solución politica o solución militar para El Salvador?," Revista ECA, April/May 1981, pp. 295.

10. Ibid., pp. 300-301.

11. Ibid., p. 302.

12. Ibid., pp. 320-321.

13. Ibid., pp. 359-360.

14. Ignacio Martín-Baró, "Acción e ideologia-psicologia social desde CA," Segunda Edición, San Salvador, UCA Editores, 1981, A Modo de Prologo, p. VI.

15. In agreement with data provided by several organizations working in this area. By 1990, the number of victims surpassed 70,000 and the population is 6 million.

16. Ignacio Martín-Baró, Ibid., Prologo, pp. VII-VIII.

17. Ibid., pp. 362-363.

18. Ibid., p. 364.

19. Ibid., p. 406.

20. Real Academia Española, 1970, pp.1259, cited by the author.

21. Ibid., p. 417.

22. Ibid., p. 417.

23. Ignacio Martín-Baró, "Acción e ideologia-psicologia social desde CA," Segunda Edición, San Salvador, UCA Editores, 1985, pp. 371.

24. Segundo Montes, "Los derechos economicos, sociales y culturales en El Salvador," Revista ECA, 476 June 1988, pp. 518-519.

25. Ibid., p. 520.

26. Ibid., pp. 523-524.

27. Ibid., p. 526.

28. Ibid., pp. 528-529.

29. Ibid., pp. 528-529.

30. Ibid., p. 534.

31. Ibid., p. 535.

32. Ibid., p. 536.

33. Ibid., p. 532.

34. Ibid., p. 537.

35. Ibid., p. 537.

36. Gianni Beretta, "Hay que darle una oportunidad a Cristiani," Interview with Ignacio Ellacuría in Pensamiento Propio, AO VII, No. 63, September 1989, pp. 49.

37. Ignacio Ellacuría "Una Nueva fase en el proceso salvadoreño," Revista ECA, No. 485, March 1989, pp. 173.

38. Gianni Beretta, "Hay que darle una oportunidad a Cristiani." Interview with Ignacio Ellacuría in Pensamiento Propio, AO VII, No. 63, September 1989

39. Ignacio Ellacuría, "Una nueva fase en el proceso salvadoreño," Revista ECA, 485, March 1989, pp. 173.

40. Ignacio Ellacuría, "Una nueva fase en el proceso salvadoreño," Revista ECA, 485, March 1989, pp. 177.

41. Gianni Beretta, "Hay que darle una oportunidad a Cristiani," Interview with Ignacio Ellacuría in Pensamiento Propio, AO VII, No. 63, September 1989.

42. Ignacio Ellacuría, "Una nueva fase en el proceso salvadoreño," Revista ECA, 485, March 1989, pp. 177.

43. "Jesuitas martires—seis vidas del pueblo," Revista Envio Instituto Historico CA, AO 8, No. 100, December 1989.

44. Revista Envio Instituto Historico CA, AO 8, No. 100, December 1989, pp. 8-9.

45. Jon Sobrino, "Sobre el asesinato de los Jesuitas salvadoreños y su concepción de la universidad," Estudios Sociales CA, Vol. I, No. 52, January - April 1990.

Part II

A Chronology of the Investigation

November 1989

11/11 FMLN offensive begins at 8:00 pm; a group of guerrillas flee through the UCA grounds after setting off a bomb at the gate in order to force it open; ten minutes later soldiers arrive and the situation is under control. (Official Statement from Jesuit Provincial)

11/11 Government radio airs accusations and death threats against Ellacuría, Segundo Montes, Archbishop Rivera, Bishop Rosa Chávez, UNTS leaders and Lutheran Bishop Medardo Gomez. (Radio Cuscatlán) Callers make statements such as, "Ellacuría is a guerrilla, his head should be cut off!" (*Proceso* 11/29/90)

11/12 Soldiers visit the Jesuit House early in the morning and collect the bomb left the night before. (Jesuit Provincial)

11/13 According to his testimony, Chief of Staff of the Armed Forces, Colonel René Emilio Ponce, orders military displacement in the zone which includes the UCA, to be coordinated by Colonel Guillermo Alfredo Benavides Moreno; the displacement begins to function in the afternoon. A section of commandos of the Atlacatl Battalion, 135 troops, is sent to reinforce the zone under the command of Lt. Espinoza Guerra and arrives at the military school at 4:00 pm. (*Proceso* 1/24/90)

11/13 The displacement includes not only soldiers of the Atlacatl but also troops from the Treasury Police, National Police and other military detachments. The zone includes the High Command, Ministry of Defense, National Intelligence Center, Military School, home of senior military officers and the UCA. (Moakley Report)

11/13 The Commando Unit of the Atlacatl Battalion ordered to the zone interrupts a special ten-day training course after only two days due to the offensive. Training was conducted by the Green Beret unit later trapped in the Sheraton Hotel during the offensive. The three lieutenants and two sergeants of the Commando Unit had been trained at Fort Benning. (Moakley Report)

11/13 Soldiers of Atlacatl Battalion search the Jesuit House at 7:00 pm, just hours after Ignacio Ellacuría returns from Spain. They continue searching other offices of the campus. Father Ellacuría invites them to return tomorrow during daylight hours but they do not come (Jesuit Provincial). The search operation is commanded by Lt. Espinoza Guerra (a 1977 graduate of the Jesuit High School, Externado San José). (*Proceso* 1/24/)

11/13 Just before entering the UCA, Lt. Héctor Ulises Cuenca Ocampo of the National Intelligence Center radios Espinoza and tells him to wait until he (Cuenca) joins the unit. (Moakley Report)

11/14 Heavy military presence all around the area of the UCA; the two entrances to the campus are guarded by soldiers. (Jesuit Provincial)

11/15 Area continues to be militarized. At mid-morning an unidentified military officer visits the Jesuits and says there will be "a lot of movement" in the afternoon or evening (Carta A Las Iglesias). Curfew begins at 6:00 pm; at 10:00 pm troops are patrolling the area (Jesuit Provincial)

11/15 Thirty Armed Forces commanders meet in the High Command from 7:30-10:30 pm to discuss the critical situation. They decide on the use of airpower, heavy artillery and cavalry units in the capitol and on a plan to assassinate guerilla leaders and destroy rebel command centers; the UCA is cited as a "launching point" for guerrilla operations. "This may have created the atmosphere that led Benavides to order the killings," according to the *Miami Herald*. The meeting ends with a prayer, holding hands; President Cristiani is called in at 10:30 pm to approve the operations personally. (MH 2/4/90)

11/15 At 10:15 pm Lt. Espinoza receives an order by radio to gather his troops together in the Military School; Espinoza has not identified the source of the order. (Moakley Report)

The following account is taken from the declarations of seven of the accused; Colonel Benavides' declarations have not been made public:

11/15 At 11:00 pm, according to declarations of the accused, Colonel Guillermo Alfredo Benavides, Director of the Military School, meets with Lt. Mendoza Vallecillos in the Operations Center and then calls Lt. Espinoza and Lt. Guevara Cerritos. He reportedly tells them, "We are going all the way . . . This is a situation in which it's them or us; we are going to begin with the leaders . . . Within our sector we have the university and Ellacuría is there." He says to Espinoza, "You have searched the place and your people know it; use the same displacement as before and you have to eliminate him and I don't want witnesses; Lt. Mendoza is going with you as head of the operation so there won't be any problems." Espinoza says, "This is very serious," and Benavides replies, "Don't worry, you have my support." Espinoza organizes his company inside the Military School; Patrols 2, 3, 4 and 6 are present; 1 and 5 had left previously so two other patrols of 15 men each from the Atlacatl Battalion are added as replacements. Espinoza calls Zarpate Castillo (of the 3rd Patrol), Molina Aguilar (of the 4th) and Gonzalez Rodriguez (6th) and two sub-sergeants and tells them they are going on a "delicate mission" . . . "to look for some priests inside the UCA . . . who are leaders of the delinquent terrorists."

11/16 At approximately 1:00 am:

The troops paint their faces, prepare equipment, then board two beige Ford pickups; Lt. Mendoza Vallecillos comes out with an AK47 and asks who can handle the weapon; all agree "Pilijay" and it is given to him. Thirty-six troops are ready to leave but not everyone fits in the trucks so some stay behind. They drive close to the UCA where they are joined by 20-25 more Atlacatl soldiers; together they walk to the UCA.

They force open the gate on the south side of the campus and enter near the Jesuit residence, leaving a security post near the entrance. Accompanied by a group of soldiers, the two lieutenants head toward the south side of the complex. They surround the rooms and begin to beat on the doors and windows. Another group heads toward the north side, led by Sgts. Pérez Vásquez and Molina Aguilar. They break the glass door into the Pastoral Center, enter the first floor and begin to burn documents. The sergeants break down a wooden door into the library.

On the other side of the complex, "Satanas" beats on the door of the house with a piece of wood for ten minutes when "a white man dressed in pajamas (Segundo Montes) opens the door and says to stop beating on the doors and windows because they understand what will happen. Satanas pulls Segundo Montes into the garden. At the other end of the building, the sleeping quarters, Pilijay tries to force the door leading to the living room. A man wearing a beige dressing gown (Father Ellacuría) comes and says, "Wait, I am going to open it but don't be creating this disorder." At the same time Lt. Mendoza moves around the outside corridor of the house. In one of the rooms he sees a woman sitting on a bed, covering another woman. It is the cook and her daughter who had asked to spend the night there because it would be safer.

At about 1:30 am, Sgt. Oscar Solórzano Esquivel "Hercules," Satanas and another soldier pull the Jesuits out of their rooms. Fathers Ellacuría, Martín Baró, Juan Ramon Moreno and Amando López begin to go to the garden. Only Martín Baró is dressed in day clothes. Hercules and another soldier go inside the building, leaving the five priests outside with Satanas and Pilijay. They are afraid the priests will overpower and disarm them so Satanas orders them face down on the ground. In this moment, Martín Baró shouts, "This is an injustice, this is an abomination!"

The two lieutenants are inside; Espinoza calls to Satanas and asks, "What are you waiting for?" Satanas returns to the Jesuits and gives Pilijay the order to shoot, "Fast, fast; do it fast!" Pilijay discharges his AK47 at Fathers Ellacuría and Martín Baró; Satanas shoots his M-16 at Montes, Moreno and Amando López. Their brains are destroyed. Espinoza orders Corporal Cotta Hérnandez to move the bodies inside. He drags the body of Father Moreno into the room of Jon Sobrino but at that moment the others are beginning to leave so he follows, leaving the other four bodies where they are. Meanwhile in the other wing of the building Sgt. Zarpate Castillo shoots Elba Julia and Marisela, according to his testimony, one bullet at a time, "to be sure they were dead and wouldn't complain." But they do not die immediately; Satanas hears some noises in the room, sees the two women and orders Pvt. Sierra Ascencio to shoot them again with his M-16.

Father Joaquin López y López, the only Salvadoran priest, is still alive. He is the oldest of all of them. At this moment he comes into the corridor, sees the bodies and returns inside. A soldier shouts at him, then shoots him. Corporal Pérez Vásquez says in his testimony, "I went to that room to search and when I passed by the man who had just been shot, I felt him grab my foot and I shot four times."

The soldiers regather in the park in front of the chapel. Lt. Guevara Cerritos shoots one bengal light and another lieutenant orders Corporal Cotta Hérnandez to shoot another as a signal for everyone to leave. As they leave they destroy the windows of the cars parked in the lot. Another group of soldiers simulates a shootout with the FMLN, with anti-tank rockets, grenades and machine-gun fire. One patrol stays another hour; Pilijay stays with them. At the gate they put up a sign saying, "The FMLN Executed the Opposition Spies. Victory or Death FMLN." As they are leaving Lt. Mendoza sees that one of Espinoza's soldiers is carrying a briefcase. They return to the Military School. Espinoza looks immediately for Colonel Benavides and says, "I am indignant about what has happened." Benavides says, "What happened? Are you worried?" "I don't like what has been done." "Be calm, don't worry. You have my support. Trust me." "I hope so, colonel."

(This reconstruction was compiled from the declarations by Proceso 1/24/90)

11/16 Around 1:00 am, according to the witness, uniformed men enter UCA.

2:30 am. Heavy gunfire and at least two bombs heard. A witness who is inside the campus sees about thirty uniformed men shooting at the Romero Chapel and the Jesuit House. (Jesuit Provincial)

The assassinated are:

Father Ignacio Ellacuría, Rector
Father Martín Baró, Vice-Rector
Father Segundo Montes, Director of IDHUCA
Father Amando López, Coordinator of Philosophy Department
Father Juan Ramon Moreno, Asst. Dir. of the Pastoral Center
Father Joaquin López y López, Director of "Fe y Alegria"
Elba Ramos, cook for the Jesuit House
Marisela Ramos, 15, her daughter

11/16   Between 5-6:00 am, the Atlacatl Unit leaves the Military School to rejoin the Battalion, located on the northern perimeter of the capitol, near the First Brigade. (Moakley Report)

11/16   At 6:00 am, according to the Moakley Report, three members of the National Intelligence Department (DNI), who witnessed the crime from a nearby building, visit the site, then report to their superiors. (Moakley Report)

11/16   Abdulio Lozano López, husband of Elba Ramos, is the first to arrive at the house. (Lawyers' Committee)

11/16   At 5:30 am, the witness, his family and UCA security guards discover the bodies.   Jorge Cerna informs the other Jesuits living in a house just off the campus. (Lawyers' Committee)

11/16   6:30 am: Jesuit Provincial, informed of the events, goes to the UCA and finds the eight bodies. The Pastoral Center is ransacked and partially burned . . . " some kind of flammable liquid was thrown over books, documents and computers that were still burning at 8:00 am." A sign is seen near the back entrance: "The   FMLN Executed the Opposition Spies. Victory or Death FMLN." Jesuits estimate the entire operation must have taken at least 1/2-hour. (Jesuit Provincial)

11/16   8:00 am: meeting of high-level intelligence officers in the DNI-CIA building; a junior officer brings news of the death of Ellacuría; everyone claps and cheers. (WP 2/6/90, MH 2/4/90)

11/16   María Julia Hérnandez, other Tutela Legal workers, the Archbishop and the press arrive at the scene of the crime.

11/16 "There is no doubt that Cristiani cannot stay in power . . . This crime removes any credibility his government may have had." (RV)

11/16 At about 8:30 am the Special Investigations Unit (SIU) arrives, "seals off the area, gathers evidence and begins to interview possible witnesses. Autopsies are performed on the victims." (US Embassy)

11/16 Ferman Cienfuegos offers condolences in the name of the FMLN General Command and calls on the North American people to demand an end to aid and a change in US policy. (RV)

11/16 Government radio reports: "The communists kill all those who don't serve them . . . The government and armed forces condemn these assassinations . . . committed by the FMLN in an attempt to destabilize democracy."

11/16 "They are the same ones who assassinated Msgr. Romero and for whom 70,000 assassinations aren't enough." At the site of the crime, Archbishop Rivera y Damas proclaims. (TV 12)

11/16 Jesuit Provincial José María Tojeira: "They were assassinated with lavish barbarity. For example, they took out their brains." (AP)

11/16 "All the sacrifices and tears and bloodshed during the long dark night by innocent people like Padre Ellacuría are not in vain . . . All the effort of a people who have fought for justice is coming to fruit . . . The hardest night comes before the most beautiful dawn . . . These are historic moments." (RV)

11/16 "This should not serve as a reason for more bloodshed . . . Their sacrifice must signify the end of the violence." Archbishop Rivera y Damas (TV 6)

11/16 Government radio network condemns the "cowardly, savage, irrational assassinations" as an attempt to "destabilize the democratic process" . . . " There is international repudiation of the FMLN."

11/16 First Brigade loudspeaker heard shouting to the troops: "Ignacio Ellacuría and Martín Baró are dead, we will continue killing communists . . . We are the soldiers of the First Brigade." Archbishop Rivera and Bishop Rosa Chávez hear the loudspeakers and report the incident to the government. (*Uno Mas Uno* 11/17)

11/16 Archbishop Rivera y Damas receives death threat saying, "You're next." (Churchworkers)

11/16 Senator Christopher Dodd: "The US government cannot continue paying for these barbarities." (CNN)

11/16 CODEHUCA: "an act of desperation and barbarity by the Armed Forces." (RV)

11/16 In Washington, Foreign Minister Pacas Castro condemns the assassinations as a "desperate act of the ultraleft." (DH 1/17)

11/16 Radio Venceremos reports that one witness survived and has identified the assassins as uniformed soldiers. (RV) *Diario Latino* says the Jesuit House was searched by "authorities" on Monday, November 13. (DL 11/16)

11/16 FMLN General Command issues statement charging the "death squads of the Armed Forces" with carrying out the executions "ordered by President Cristiani and the High Command." (RV)

11/16 US Ambassador William Walker says, "It is difficult for me to imagine what kind of beasts would assassinate six priests and other innocent victims in cold blood . . . This is a criminal act of such repugnance that to say we condemn and deplore it would be inadequate." (LPG 11/17/89)

11/16 CNN News to El Salvador censored during reports of the massacre. (CNN)

11/16 President Cristiani condemns the assassinations which "complicate the critical situation" and were carried out by "groups who want to block the dialogue process"; he has ordered a full investigation but says it is unfortunate that a witness who survived "hasn't been available for our investigators to question." (CIN)

11/17 First Brigade deserter, César Joya Mártinez tells US press that the First Brigade and all other military installations and security forces "have the necessary apparatus to carry out assassinations . . . The *modus operandi* (of the Jesuit killings) is typical of the death squads." (RV)

11/17 Joaquin Villalobos: "It was a bad calculation on the part of the Armed Forces and Cristiani . . . They understood the high political cost but believed it would be worth the price . . . During the night of the 15th-16th they raided houses and offices of the popular movement with the intention of eliminating the political opposition; almost everyone had taken precautions and was in hiding, but the Jesuits remained in their house because Cristiani had assured them a few days earlier, they would be safe. "They thought they were going to win the war that night and they wanted to assure the political stability of the country . . . Cristiani knew and probably the U.S. Ambassador knew . . . and believed it was necessary to control the country . . . But it reversed on them and will provoke the total isolation of the government . . . It was their suicide, a serious error. Why were the Jesuits killed? They contributed enormously to the education of our people, to the political debate, to an understanding of the need for political pluralism . . . The Armed Forces and the oligarchy don't support intelligence, reason or debate." (RV)

11/17 ANEP (National Association of Private Enterprise) condemns the assassinations and congratulates the Armed Forces on their "professional attitude" in avoiding greater loss of life; calls on the national and international press to "be objective to avoid confusion which the enemies of the homeland take advantage of." (DH 11/17/89)

11/17 U.S. Ambassador Walker says four US pathologists are coming to the country to examine the bodies; the US is "looking for witnesses and will guarantee their security," he says . . . "The guerrillas have the responsibility to end the violence . . . They don't have any popular support." (TV 12)

11/17 "US pathologists view the bodies and review the autopsy reports. In a preliminary assessment, they conclude the SIU is performing a competent investigation and that the autopsies are thorough and professional." (US Embassy Report)

11/18 Private service held in the UCA for friends, co-workers and families of those slain.   The Chapel is badly damaged, photos of Archbishop Romero full of bullet holes. (Interview)

11/18 Press receives copy of letter written by the Attorney General to the Pope, asking that he remove Bishops Rivera and Rosa Chávez "for their own safety." He also denounces the "popular church." (Letter)

11/18 State Department spokesperson: "Unfortunately when someone tries to take power by bullets instead of by ballots, sometimes innocent people are affected." (DL)

11/18 María Julia Hérnandez: "There is more than sufficient evidence to determine who is responsible." (TV 12)

11/18 The Jesuit community will wait only weeks for a complete investigation . . . " We will not allow this crime to go unpunished for ten years like the assassination of Archbishop Romero." (TV 12)

11/19 Archbishop Rivera y Damas:" The assassins are from the Armed Forces or close to them." During the Sunday Homily he denounces the "irresponsible campaign in the media" and against the Jesuits, particularly against Ellacuría which led up to the assassinations. He says Cristiani and the High Command "have publicly sworn their commitment to investigate," and also condemns the "excessive force" used by the Armed Forces in response to the offensive. (TV 12)

11/19 Mass and burial service presided over by the Archbishop; Lutheran Bishop Medardo Gomez says, "There is no pardon from God for this crime." President Cristiani, Ambassador Walker, Rubén Zamora, Humberto Centeno and hundreds of others attend the service. Walker says "there is no concrete proof" of responsibility for the massacre. (TV 12)

11/20 Lucia Barrera de Cerna returns to the UCA for the first time after staying with relatives in another part of the city. She relates her testimony to María Julia Hérnandez of Tutela Legal and is advised to seek refuge in an embassy. She goes immediately to the Spanish Embassy and sends a note for her husband and child to join her. (Lawyers' Committee for Human Rights)

11/20 María Julia Hérnandez says the investigation is "advancing rapidly." (TV 12)

11/22 "FBI agent arrives to provide technical assistance to the SIU and to receive a briefing on the investigation." (US Embassy Report)

11/22-23 Witness Lucia Barrera de Cerna testifies to the Attorney General and members of the Special Investigation Commission, then leaves for Miami accompanied by diplomats, her husband Jorge and her 4-year-old daughter Gerardina. The family is held in Miami by the FBI until December 3rd. (Lawyers' Committee)

11/23 "Embassy is advised that a possible eye-witness to the murders, Lucia Barrera de Cerna, is leaving El Salvador for the US for security reasons, with the assistance of the French and Spanish Embassies. Embassy legal officer and FBI agent accompany Mrs. Cerna to Miami in a French military aircraft, after State Department arranges air clearance and immigration authorization. Party is met by French and Spanish consuls and local Jesuits. The Jesuits express concerns about security and it is agreed to meet the next day, after the Cernas have completed immigration documentation." (US Embassy Report)

11/23 During Embassy press conference Ambassador Walker announces the findings of the three forensics experts. Dr. Richard Kirschner, C. Swan and Dr. J. Fitzpatrick determined the victims were not tortured and were killed with high power bullets. (DH 11/24/89)

11/24 - 12/1 "The SIU Director (Lt. Col. Manuel Antonio Rivas Mejia) and polygrapher arrive in Miami. Mrs. Cerna and her husband are questioned at FBI headquarters by the SIU Director and FBI agents. The Cernas give contradictory versions of what they may have heard and/or seen the night of the murders. After the interviews the Jesuit community assumes responsibility for the Cernas." (US Embassy Report)

11/25 The Attorney General says there is "no indication as to whether the assassinations were carried out by the army, terrorists or private persons." (EM) The Jesuit Provincial accuses the Attorney General of "spending more time trying to discredit witnesses" than in conducting a serious investigation. (RV)

11/28 Tutela Legal issues official report of the Archdiocese:

1. The operation lasted at least one hour.

2. There was a large group of uniformed soldiers; the witness saw a group of approximately five uniformed persons at the same time, she heard shooting, glass breaking, doors opening and closing; five persons entered by one door (on the west side of the building); others entered the door on the northeast side and still another group entered the Pastoral Center which was searched and burned with flame throwers.

3. Military Intelligence was well-acquainted with the premises which had been meticulously searched by uniformed soldiers on November 13.

4. The location was heavily guarded with permanent posts in the Torre Democracia, Colonia Militar Manuel José Arce, north gate of the UCA, around the periphery of the campus, in La Ceiba de Guadalupe and in the area of Jardines de Guadalupe.

5. In spite of the militarization of the area, the curfew and the heavy gunfire from within the UCA, "the Armed Forces did not respond as it would have in the case of an FMLN action, which means knowledge of the operation on the part of the troops located in the radius of security of the High Command, the Colonia Militar. All evidence . . . establishes that those responsible . . . were members of the military belonging to the Armed Forces." (Tutela Legal)

11/29 Father Jon Sobrino: "I hope that those who now promise an investigation in order to give an appearance of normalcy and democracy also investigate why there have never been nor could have been serious investigations in El Salvador before . . . That this will not be a cover-up to distract attention from the 70, 000 cases that must be investigated . . . or an excuse to say things are better in El Salvador. . . . Who in the world has really worked for an investigation of El Mozóte or Sumpúl or, more recently, the October 31 assassination of ten unionists in broad daylight?" (Sobrino Paper 11/29/89)

11/30 "The Embassy establishes a task force to formally coordinate ongoing US Government assistance to the Jesuit investigation." (US Embassy Report)

December 1989

12/1 Dr. Miguel Francisco Estrada, Dean of the Faculty of Business Administration, will replace Dr. Ellacuría as Rector of the UCA. (DL 12/1)

12/1 General Maxwell Thurmond meets with the High Command and reportedly says, "There is only one way out of this . . . if some of your people were involved in the Jesuit murders, cough them up." (NYT 1/21/90)

12/1 "Ambassador Walker, accompanied by US Southern Command General, Commander General Thurman, stresses the importance of a thorough investigation into the Jesuit killings to the Salvadoran military high command." (US Embassy Report)

12/3 Bishop Rosa Chávez: "There are names of people implicated . . . If they want to tell the truth it can be known." (TV 12)

12/3 "Young Officers' Letter" accuses Treasury Police Commander Héctor Heriberto Hérnandez with responsibility for ordering the assassinations, Captain Alfonso Chávez Garcia of carrying out the order. (Letter)

12/3 Lawyers' Committee interviews Lucia Barrera de Cerna in Miami; the family is taken to another city, under the care of the Jesuits.

12/4 Colonel Hérnandez denies the charges and accuses the FMLN of assassinating the Jesuits . . . "They entered the UCA that day before the curfew . . . They could have been former students, it's possible . . . They are just trying to divide the government . . . We are trying to save El

Salvador, not to endanger the country . . . The extremists are discrediting a large number of officers." (TV 12)

12/4 "Embassy officials meet with Roberto D'Aubuisson to discuss media reports of his possible responsibility for the killings. He denies any involvement and promises full support for the investigation, including his willingness to be polygraphed." (US Embassy Report)

12/5 Special Investigations Unit asks High Command to provide a list of the troops who searched the UCA on December 13. (Moakley Report)

12/6 "Due to the circumstances in which it occurred, the assassination of the Jesuits has become a critical test for the viability of democracy in El Salvador . . . A democracy which is not only ritual elections . . . but also means satisfaction of the material needs of the popular majority, it also implies . . . respect for human rights, an efficient legal system and institutional subordination of the Armed Forces to the civilian power . . . The uncovering of this case puts all these elements into play." (*Proceso* 12/6/89)

12/6 Colonel Ponce denies any connection between the assassins and the Armed Forces "as an institution." "We are willing to be investigated." (TV 12)

12/7 Attorney General "laments" the decision "of some Bishops" not to allow a representative of the Church to participate in the commission to investigate the assassinations. (TV 2) He accuses the Church of "blocking the investigation." (TV 6, 12)

12/8 The Archbishop says the Attorney General is "biased." "He seems to be defending those accused of the crime." "There are very serious things blocking the investigation." (TV 12)

12/8 Colonel Elena Fuentes says the government "has a special interest in uncovering these crimes committed by the FMLN." [the murder of the Jesuits and the FENASTRAS bombing.] (DH 12/8/89)

12/8 "The killings were part of an effort to discredit the Government and the Armed Forces," says President Cristiani. He reports that investigators from Scotland Yard, the FBI, Spain and Costa Rica are assisting the Special Investigations Unit and announces the government will offer a $250,000 reward to any informant who "unconsciously or against their will" participated in the crime; the person and his family group will be provided with security in another country and will be exonerated. During the past week the FBI has been investigating the Armed Forces, now has a list of names of all soldiers who were in the area. He says that Colonel Hérnandez and Captain Chávez are both "willing to be investigated." (TV 12)

12/10 Paul Tipton, President of the Association of Jesuit Colleges and Universities, writes to Secretary of State James Baker saying, "We have been reliably informed that the US Ambassador to El Salvador, William Walker, and other members of the Embassy staff have been asserting to reporters and others in El Salvador that the testimony of the witness is of no value. We further understand from very reliable sources that a US official said Tutela Legal . . . had instructed the witness to fabricate her testimony. Neither assertion of Ambassador Walker is true . . . His apparent participation in efforts to discredit the testimony of this courageous witness is a shocking betrayal of the responsibilities of our official representative in El Salvador . . . and . . . raises serious questions regarding the commitment of this administration to the objective of a fair, thorough, and impartial investigation of the murders." (Letter)

12/10 Archbishop Rivera y Damas accuses the US Embassy of not providing protection promised to the witness, Lucia Barrera de Cerna; he says she was "aggressively and violently" interrogated in Miami . . . "She vacillated and withdrew the declaration she had made in El Salvador . . . Now that she is free from the pressures of her 'protectors' she has returned to the truth" ; according to the Archbishop, the Jesuits will issue a report with the names of the people who threatened the witness, including the threat of deportation.

He also responds to charges made by the Attorney General that the Church is blocking the investigation, saying, "Let's be serious . . . We are not blocking the investigation." He says he was not in the country when Auxiliary Bishop Rosa Chávez made the decision not to allow Church participation in the government investigation commission but he supports the decision . . . the Vicar General and Rosa Chávez "acted wisely and prudently." (TV 6, 12)

12/10 "The SIU completes interviewing all officers commanding units in the University area the night of the killings." (US Embassy Report)

12/11 "The SIU establishes a hotline for anonymous callers having information on the murders." (US Embassy Report)

12/11 "The SIU identifies the army unit that had conducted a search of the University on November 13, three nights before the murders. The unit is part of the Atlacatl immediate reaction battalion and was under the temporary operational control of Colonel Guillermo Benavides, Director of the Military Academy." (US Embassy Report)

12/11 "The SIU begins polygraphing soldiers from the units stationed in the area the night of the crime. It also identifies the lot number of the bullets used in the murders." (US Embassy Report)

12/11 Lucia Barrera story released in US and Salvadoran press. *Diario De Hoy* reports that she "changed her testimony three times" and has had six lie detector tests . . . " She was upset and confused in spite of efforts by the FBI to calm and reassure her"; Jesuit Provincial José María Tojeira says, "She was in the hands of the FBI during many days and we have solid proof that she was mistreated . . . Personally, I think she was psychologically tortured"; the article quotes Ambassador Walker as saying US policy could be threatened, "if the mystery that surrounds the assassinations is not resolved"; responding to the Archbishop's charges yesterday he says, "It hurts me that the Archbishop does not believe that the Government of the United States and he are in the same search for the truth." (DH 12/11/89)

12/11 Attorney General Colorado is "surprised" by the Archbishop's charges . . . "The Spanish Ambassador can testify as to how she was treated here . . . I don't know how she was treated in the U.S."; he questions the motives of the Catholic hierarchy, saying, "I know the Bishop has a brother in the guerrilla"; announces that he will call Fidel Chávez-Mena, María Julia Hérnandez and possibly the Archbishop to make declarations this week. (TV 6)

12/11 State Department issues statement saying the Archbishop "was misinformed" about the treatment of the witness. "She was well-treated." (TV 6)

12/12 Vice-Minister of Security Colonel Montano says Colonel Ponce has given a sworn declaration to the Attorney General on the case and that Colonel Heriberto Hérnandez "has been investigated." (YSU) He also alleges that the FMLN is responsible for the crime, "They knew they were defeated by November 16 so they carried out the assassinations." (TV 12) He accuses María Julia Hérnandez of "counseling the witness to say the assassins were military" and accuses the Bishops of "sympathy with the terrorist left." (DH 12/13/89)

12/12 Jesuits of El Salvador release statement deploring the investigation and the treatment of the witness by U.S. officials. "We especially thank the churches, governments, academic institutions, the press and endless numbers of friends who have supported the Jesuits before, during and after the crime . . . We are convinced that without this solidarity, the assassination of our brothers would have fallen into the anonymous impunity that has characterized so many crimes in our country . . . We wish to thank the Archbishop . . . for his support in this case. Without his technical help at the time of the investigation and his spiritual words, the sad road we have had to take since the unjust deaths of our brothers would have been much more difficult." (Communiqué)

12/14 María Julia Hérnandez summoned to court to give sworn testimony on the case. She later tells the press, "I could only testify to what I saw and heard at the site of the crime . . . The Church presented its official document which concluded that elements of the Armed Forces were implicated." Instead of being questioned about the crime she was interrogated about her investigation. "I took two bullet shells lying next to the body of Father Ellacuría and two from the room where the employees were . . . The Attorney General says this is a crime." (TV 12)

12/14 The Attorney General will ask the Bishops' Conference (CEDES) to investigate the Bishops and María Julia Hérnandez for "obstructing justice"; he lambasts the attitude of the Church and says there are no "important indications" as to responsibility for the assassinations. (TV 12)

He says the fact that María Julia Hérnandez affirmed she had "collected objects" without legal authority is a crime. "Everyone knows that the scene of a crime is sacred . . . This, added to the strange attitude of the Bishops . . . leads one to assume intent to block the investigation." (DH 12/15/90)

12/15 Asked if she is afraid for her life, María Julia replies, "All Salvadorans live in unstable conditions due to the circumstances here in El Salvador." Her declaration yesterday was taken in the presence of Judge Dr. Ricardo Zamora and Saul Zelaya Castillo and Carlos Figeac, of the Attorney General's office. (EM)

12/15 Dr. Fidel Chávez-Mena did not appear to testify today. (TV 6)

12/15 "The SIU reports having conducted 147 interviews of soldiers and have reviewed over 300 ballistics tests on the weapons of soldiers who were near the University on November 16." (U.S. Embassy Report)

12/16 One month after the assassinations; Radio Venceremos comments, "Instead of investigating the crime they are attempting to discredit the witnesses . . . They are not going to punish this crime . . . It is a crime of the government . . . Even if Héctor Heriberto Hérnandez were to be tried he is only one of the Tandona . . . Staben, Guzmán, Aguilar, Fuentes, . . . They are all guilty." (RV)

12/16 Thirty-day Mass held in the UCA Chapel; the new Rector of the UCA, Father Francisco Javier Estrada thanks the hundreds of participants "for your courage in coming today." Archbishop Rivera presides over the Mass. (TV 12)

12/16 Two Spanish detectives will arrive in the country Monday to pursue the investigation "at the request of the government." (TV 12)

12/16 "The police officials sent by the Spanish Government to monitor the investigation depart El Salvador. They report that the SIU is conducting an objective, professional and thorough investigation." (US Embassy Report)

12/16 The Archbishop warns that the "laws of the Church" could be applied against the Attorney General if he continues threatening the Church and "creating a smoke screen around the assassinations." (Sonora)

12/18 MAC Deputy Guillermo Lacayo returns from government mission to the U.S. saying the issue of the Jesuits is primary . . . "Religious sectors are giving false information . . . Aid will be discussed in January and they are going to demand an end to military aid; he says there are two hypotheses about the assassinations, one is that the extreme right is responsible, the other is the FMLN . . . Neither of these possibilities can be discarded." (TV 6)

12/19 Meeting arranged by Armed Forces investigators between the Jesuits (Padres Tojeira and Estrada) and Colonel Ponce "in an effort to reduce tensions." Colonel Carlos Avilés, educated by the Jesuits, participates in the meeting. (Moakley Report) Avilés, head of Psychological Operations for the High Command, previously served as head of the Special Investigations Unit. (Moakley Report)

12/20 Colonel Carlos Armando Avilés, Head of Psychological Operations for the Armed Forces, informs his friend, U.S. advisor Major Eric Buckland, that Colonel Benavides is a suspect in the case. Buckland fails to inform his superiors. (MH 1/16/90)

Avilés allegedly tells Buckland the information is only to be used "in case of emergency." According to Buckland, Avilés says his information is based on a conversation with Col. López y López, another ex-director of the Special Investigations Unit who was assigned early in December to assist Lt. Col. Rivas in the investigation. According to Avilés, Benavides approached Rivas early in the investigation and said, "I did it . . . What can you do to help me? What can we do about this?" (Moakley Report)

12/20-30 During a ten-day period Major Buckland informs two people of what he knows, information to be used "only in case of emergency." (Moakley Report))

12/20-22 "A member of the U.S. Military Group in El Salvador receives third-hand information implicating Colonel Benavides as the intellectual author of the murders. The U.S. military officer does not pass this information to his superior officer." (U.S. Embassy Report)

12/22 "Colonel Avilés, Father Tojeira and Father Estrada receive a full and detailed briefing on the progress in the investigation." (U.S. Embassy Report)

12/22 Editorial in *Diario De Hoy* criticizes the Bishops as a result of the investigation . . . "What's Happening With THOSE Bishops?".. "Why are 'these people' listened to when they are only trying to discredit the Armed Forces? . . . Why do they threaten to excommunicate the Attorney General simply because he hasn't taken part in the campaign to discredit the Armed Forces? Which genocidal terrorists have been threatened with excommunication? . . . We have had enough damage by the Catholic Church . . . of using the pulpit to preach hatred and violence . . . of confusing the humble people with their insane preaching." (DH 12/22)

12/27 Conservative Bishop Romeo Tovar Astorga returns from Rome where he met with the Pope; he says there is an "enormous disinformation campaign. "It is a mistake," he says, "to reduce all the deaths to the case of the Jesuits." (TV 6, 12)

12/27 Jesuit Superior General Peter Hans Kolvenbach arrives in the country for a three-day private visit. (TV 12) "He meets with President Cristiani and receives a briefing from the SIU." (U.S. Embassy Report)

12/28 "We don't want political bishops," says the Attorney General in another letter attacking the Bishops, this time to CEDES: "We don't want reports of death or judges who lack scientific proof, who issue sentences on the basis of suspicions . . . We don't want the Church to be mixed up in social conflicts . . . There is a subtle link in the Church from evangelization to consciousness-raising to politization." (DH 12/28/89)

On 12/31 the paper continues the publication of the letter: "They are not investigators . . . As of this date the teams of the FBI, Spanish, and Canadian police have been unable to arrive at definite conclusions . . .

How could the Archbishop, only three days after the crime, accuse some-one? It is not his field, his jurisdiction nor his mission . . . María Julia Hérnandez is not a competent authority . . . She did not have the right to take four bullet shells from the site of the crime." (DH 12/31)

12/28 "An FBI polygraph expert performs quality control checks on the SIU's polygraph tests." (U.S. Embassy Report) The ballistics experts find similarities between the bullets found in the UCA and those belonging to the Atlacatl troops. (Moakley Report)

12/30 Air Force General Juan Rafael Bustillo says, "The Church is unfortunately misled . . . especially Bishops Rivera and Rosa Chávez. Those two gentlemen are mistaken in their mission as pastors . . . They play the role of useful fools for the FMLN." (TV 6)

January 1990

1/2 "The Milgroup officer tells his superior of the information he received implicating Colonel Benavides. Colonel Menjívar, the Milgroup Commander, and an Embassy political officer report this information to Salvadoran Chief of Staff Colonel Ponce." (U.S. Embassy Report)

1/2 Major Eric Buckland reports his conversation with Colonel Avilés to his superior, Colonel Militon Menjívar, the head of the U.S. Milgroup. (MH 2/4/90) Menjívar and another U.S. official confront Ponce with the information. Ponce calls Avilés into a meeting of the High Command; Avilés denies the charges of passing the information and submits to a lie detector test.

1/2 According to the Moakley Report, Major Buckland confides to his superior officer, Colonel William Hunter, his conversation with Avilés; Hunter immediately reports to Menjívar who, without notifying the Ambassador or Deputy Chief of Mission, but in the company of a political officer, goes directly to Colonel Ponce with the information; Ponce demands to know the identity of the source. Avilés and Buckland are summoned to the High Command; Avilés admits talking with Buckland but denies saying anything about the alleged conversation with Lt. Col. Rivas saying, "If I had known this, would I have risked my career telling it to the Major?" (Moakley Report)

1/2 Scotland Yard detectives arrive in the country.

1/2 President Cristiani says there have been "great advances" in the investigation, now focusing on the Armed Forces. "For the first time in our history a scientific investigation is being conducted." Colonel Ponce has provided a list of all military personnel in the area on the night of the crime and ballistics tests have been performed on their weapons . . . " FMLN participation has been discounted." (TV 6, 12, EM, DL, DH)

1/2 "President Cristiani reiterates that the focus of the SIU's investigation is on the military." (U.S. Embassy Report)

1/2 Ambassador Walker tells Congressional investigators "there is no evidence to implicate the military," and asserts that the killers "could have been guerrillas dressed in army uniforms." (NYT 1/21)

1/3 "The prosecutors and judge assigned to the case begin to review the SIU's evidence." (U.S. Embassy Report)

1/3 Colonel Menjívar makes a presentation to the High Command about the accusations; Deputy Chief of Mission Jeffrey Dietrich meets with Cristiani and makes the same presentation. Buckland writes a sworn declaration which is presented to the Minister of Defense and the High Command. An Embassy official meets with Col. Rivas who denies any conversation with Benavides. Colonel López y López also denies any conversation with Rivas or Avilés on the subject. (Moakley Report)

1/5 Eight members of the military are formally arrested. (TV 12)

1/5 Major Buckland is given a lie detector test by the FBI; Avilés is also tested by Salvadoran authorities; results demonstrate a certain degree of "deception" in both cases. (Moakley Report)

1/6 Major Buckland leaves for the U.S., where he takes additional lie detector tests. (Moakley Report)

1/6 "Scotland Yard sends a team to review developments in the investigation . . . " (U.S. Embassy Report)

1/7 Cristiani goes on national television and in a brief, 4-minute address says the case has been broken; he announces that an Honor Commission of the Armed Forces "will determine the exact circumstances of the assassinations and uncover the truth in all its magnitude." The Criminal Investigations Unit has concluded that "some elements of the Armed Forces" were involved. "The Armed Forces will not allow any of its members to impugn its professionalism and its morale." The President repeats the reward offer and says, "I want the world to know that I have no commitment to anyone except the Salvadoran people." (National Network)

1/7 "President Cristiani announces that the SIU has developed evidence implicating members of the Atlacatl unit in the murders. Two officers and 45 enlisted men in the unit are ordered confined to barracks. President Cristiani also announces the formation of a special military honor board to review the SIU's evidence." (U.S. Embassy)

A reporter calls Colonel Ponce just before Cristiani's speech to confirm rumors that 45 soldiers and five officers of the Atlacatl Battalion have been detained; Ponce won't confirm or deny the story but admits some troops have been asked to stay in the barracks, "to be available to the Investigations Commission." They are believed to be the troops who participated in the search of the Jesuit House on November 13. (Interview)

1/7-13 Honor Commission meets to review the evidence. Moakley investigation unable to determine exactly what occurs during this week. (Moakley Report)

1/8 Cristiani confirms detentions of five officers and five soldiers. (TV 12)

1/8 Spokesperson for the White House expresses "satisfaction" with the progress. "We are very content . . . Cristiani has shown great courage." (YSU)

1/8 Rector of the UCA says he is confident of Cristiani's goodwill, but that it is essential for him to take the next step and make the names public. (YSU) "This is transcendental but still incomplete . . . We don't have the authors of the crime, we only know they belong to the institution . . . It is nothing new until we have the names and prosecution of those responsible." (TV 12)

1/8 Husband of slain employee, Julia Ramos, says, "It is important that it be uncovered . . . but if they investigate or not it really doesn't matter." Ramos has returned to work at the UCA in spite of concerns for his safety; he was on the premises the night of the massacre, when both his wife and daughter were slain. (TV 6)

1/8 Assembly President Valdivieso says the crime was not "institutional . . . It's worth it to purify the army in order to save it." (YSU, TV 6)

1/8 Attorney General again cites Fidel Chávez Mena and Bishop Rosa Chávez to appear and present declarations, both because of statements they have made implicating the military. (TV 6)

1/8 Minister of Defense Larios says, "No comment." (TV 12)

1/8-10 "Staff members of the House Task Force on the Jesuit murders investigation visit El Salvador." (U.S. Embassy Report)

1/9 "A U.S. Department of Justice expert provides quality control on the SIU's ballistics tests." (U.S. Embassy Report)

1/9 *Washington Post.* "It is laudable . . . although doubtful they will be prosecuted." (1/9/90)

1/9 In Bonn, Archbishop Rivera says, "The fact that he has uncovered to a certain point those guilty . . . is something we must celebrate . . . There have been many crimes that have been forgotten." (DL 1/9)

1/9 Minister of Information, Mauricio Sandoval says 115 members of the armed forces have been interviewed, 103 civilians; he says the case will be resolved within 72 hours "as long as there are no obstacles." Seven or eight persons carried out the operation, "in the presence of uniformed personnel." The victims were not tortured; 230 bullet casings were found from AK 47s, M-16s, M-60 grenade launchers and Low anti-tank weapons. According to the report, one group assassinated the Jesuits, another killed Julia and Marisela Ramos with different weapons. Sandoval does not reveal any names. (TV 6, 12, YSU, EM, DL)

1/9 An unidentified military officer says the army supports the investigation but that all information will come from the Presidential Palace because, "We don't want interested parties to jeopardize the investigation . . . or anyone to think the army is exerting pressure." (DH 1/10/90)

1/9 "The Church is not interested in knowing who they are, only to know the truth for the sole reason it would mean the end of impunity in El Salvador," says Bishop Rosa Chávez. "It could be the basis for the purification (of the Armed Forces) and for justice in the country." He recognizes Cristiani's courage and says he has the support "of a good number of military officers." (TV 6, 12)

1/9 "Auxiliary Bishop Msgr. Rosa Chávez publicly states that he and the Catholic Church are satisfied with the progress in the investigation." (U.S. Embassy Report)

1/9 Attorney General Colorado says, "Tutela Legal hasn't helped at all . . . We had to eliminate the damage done in order to arrive at a scientific conclusion." (TV 6, 12)

1/9 *Diario De Hoy* comments on the investigation as "demonstrating the will of the government to reestablish law and order . . . This proves that the supreme authorities and the Army . . . are removed from abuses and attacks that have been committed by individuals and groups who act outside the law . . . These actions . . . are, however, a result of the atrocities and the climate of barbarity let loose by the terrorism. In the two decades since the formation of the first subversive movements, with the indirect but decisive participation of the universities and certain sectors of the clergy, [we have suffered] civil disobedience, lack of respect for the law . . . and attacks against morals . . . It would be absurd to differentiate morally between one class of terrorism and another." (DH 1/9/90)

1/10 President Cristiani meets briefly with the press and says the At-lacatl troops are not under arrest but "concentrated" in the barracks for the investigation. He gives no names and tells reporters, "You have to understand this is a very delicate case." (TV 6)

1/10 Senators Christopher Dodd and John Warner meet with the President, Ponce and others. Dodd says, "No one has given me any names . . . Ponce and the others say they are not afraid . . . It is impossible for me to believe that two lieutenants and 45 soldiers are responsible . . . This must be investigated completely." (TV 6, 12)

1/10 Retired Colonel Ochóa Pérez says, "The military who gave the orders to commit this Machiavellian crime must be discovered . . . The material and intellectual authors must be punished." (TV 6)

1/11 Reuters reports that Colonel Alfredo Benavides, Director of the Military School, is under investigation. (DL 1/11/90)

1/11 Dr. Fidel Chávez Mena presents a sworn declaration; says he has no concrete information. "I just made hypothetical political statements." (TV 6)

1/11 "Supreme Court President Mauricio Gutierrez publicly applauds the investigation and assures that the accused will receive a fair trial. If found guilty they will be punished, whether they are civilians, military or influential people, he is reported saying in a local journal." (U.S. Embassy Report)

1/12 Dr. Miguel Francisco Estrada, Rector of the UCA, clarifies his position on the progress of the investigation. "It is positive," he says, in that it is a step forward toward justice, "an indispensable requirement for peace." It proves that Cristiani has more than just "good intentions" and shows that the Armed Forces wishes to comply with its "primary mission . . . to protect the citizenry even when the transgressors are members of its own body." The investigation is not yet complete, however . . . "It will be complete when the names of the intellectual and material authors are known and they receive the full weight of the law." He suggests the President intervened in the case because of international pressure, the threat of U.S. aid cuts, his own "ethical disposition," and because the crime "compromises the identity and essence of the army, created to defend citizens, not to assassinate them." (EM 1/12/90)

1/12 Reporters wait all day for an announcement from the President; late in the afternoon, Secretary of Information Mauricio Sandoval says, "the time frame [72 hours] was taken too literally." He denies rumors of military pressure or a coup d'état. (YSU)

1/13 Extrajudicial declarations are taken from the eight men in custody. (DL 1/22/90)

1/13 *Los Angeles Times* reports that two colonels have been "confined to base," Colonel Benavides and Colonel Carlos Armando Aviles, head of Psychological Operations, who allegedly leaked Benavides' name to the Embassy. Aviles had just been promoted to Military Attaché in Washington on January 1st, but that order has been cancelled. Apparently Benavides spoke to Aviles, Aviles to U.S. officials and U.S. officials confronted Ponce with the information. An "embarrassed and furious" Ponce ordered Avils to submit to a lie detector test which he failed. The article reports tensions within the military as "extremely high. . . . "The grounding of Avils illustrates that within the military there were sharp divisions opening up . . . very sharp divisions." (MH 1/13/90)

1/13 President Cristiani gives a four-minute pre-taped television and radio address to "reveal the results of the investigation." He says the following persons have been "placed at the disposition of the judicial system" :

> Colonel Guillermo Alfredo Benavides Moreno, 44
> Director, Military School "General Gerardo Barrios"
> Lt. José Ricardo Espinosa Guerra, 28
> Company Commander of a commando unit of the Atlacatl Battalion
> Lt. Yusshy René Mendoza Vallecillos, 26
> Section Commander, Military School 1st Lt.
> Gonzalo Guevara Cerritos, 27
> Member of Commando Unit Atlacatl Battalion
> Sgt. Antonio Ramiro Avalos Vargas," Satanas", 21
> Member of Commando Unit
> Sgt. Tomás Zapata Castillo, 28
> Member of Commando Unit
> Corporal Angel Pérez Vasquez, 30
> Member of Commando Unit
> Pvt. Oscar Mariano Amaya Grimaldi, "Pilijay", 26
> Member of Commando Unit
> Pvt. Jorge Alberto Sierra Ascencio (who deserted in December)
> Member of Commando Unit

He says the investigation was conducted by the Special Criminal Investigation Unit with the assistance of investigators from the U.S., Spain, Great Britain and Canada "who worked with total freedom . . . and have examined the data impartially and professionally . . . responding to the demand of the Salvadoran people for application of the law." Cris-

tiani, flanked by Minister of Defense Larios, Chief of Staff Colonel
Ponce, Vice-Ministers of Defense and Security, Colonels Montano and
Zépeda and Colonel Gilberto Rubio, says the Armed Forces Honor Com-
mission has reviewed the case and it will now go to the criminal court.
(National Network)

1/14 *New York Times* reports "widespread rumors of a coup last week
were checked by the U.S. Embassy." Officials of State and Defense "attempted to squelch rumors" that a U.S. advisor knew about the planning
of the assassinations saying, "There is no evidence that a U.S. military
officer had advance knowledge." The unnamed officer has been sent back
to the U.S. and is reportedly being interrogated by U.S. officials. According to the report, the officer knew about the involvement of Colonel
Benavides but did not report it to the U.S., "because it was already
known by the Salvadorans." (1/14/90)

1/14 "Colonel Benavides did not give the order and probably never
even knew about it," says Radio Venceremos. "He is charged because
the massacre occurred in a sector under his responsibility that night but
he is an *institutionalista*, not an officer, who has participated in repressive
actions . . . This was not a personal decision but part of premeditated
counterinsurgency operations . . . Benavides will eventually be released
and sent to exile." (RV)

1/15 Rosa Chávez: "They insist it was simply a group of members of
the Armed Forces that have stained the honor of the institution . . . It is
difficult for us to accept this assertion . . . It is not enough to punish just
a few . . . We must see who really are the enemies of the people and of
the nation." (TV 12)

1/15 Criminal Court Judge Ricardo Zamora will hear the case against
the accused; if he decrees sufficient merit to proceed with the prosecution
they will lose their military status and be sent to Mariona Prison to await
trial. Zamora is the Judge because he was on duty the night of the crime.
(EM 1/15/90)

1/15 ARENA President Armando Calderon Sol says the investigation
should go "all the way" but that the institution should not be implicated.
He implies that a thorough investigation would go "all the way to the

FMLN. . . . "It has the ramifications of a conspiracy between members of the military and the FMLN." (TV 6)

1/15 Foreign Minister Pacas Castro announces that the visit of Cristiani to the U.S., scheduled to begin tomorrow, will be postponed, allegedly because the UN Secretary General is in Moscow. Cristiani will depart on January 30. "The postponement doesn't have anything to do with the assassinations." (YSU)

1/16 Vice-President Merino responds to the "conspiracy theory" saying, "it is illogical that the government or military would have been involved in such a crime that could destabilize the government . . . The motives must be understood and the theory of a conspiracy studied . . . Perhaps the crime was not committed in coordination with the FMLN but the effects are the same." (YSU)

1/16 Exactly two months after the crime, eight members of the Armed Forces appear in court at 3:30 pm under very tight security. Colonel Juan Carlos Schlenker of the National Guard escorts Colonel Benavides. Benavides testifies for two hours and twenty minutes, and reportedly denies all charges, both extrajudicially and judicially. Judge Ricardo Zamora receives declarations from one of the other officers before everyone leaves at 7:30 pm. The Judge has three days to determine if there is sufficient evidence to bind the accused over for trial. (YSU, Sonora, TV 6, 12)

1/16 "This is not an isolated case but the product of an ideological conception," says Archbishop Rivera, "others could be implicated. We'll see if things continue with the same spirit." (TV 12)

1/16 Cristiani holds press conference for several international reporters and informs them that the two lieutenants have accused Benavides of ordering the assassinations, that no officers of higher rank will be charged with knowledge of the crime. "I think most of it is covered." The motive, he says, "is unclear." "The killings stemmed from a feeling shared by many in the army that the Jesuits were helping the rebels . . . These guys could have felt that they were part of the offensive." A Latin American diplomat says, "Benavides is the scapegoat . . . He's the one who is taking responsibility . . . but there was a top man who knew about it and ordered it." (NYT 1/18/90)

1/17 The investigation "is a question of national survival," says *Diario De Hoy* . . . " President Cristiani deserves support to prosecute those responsible, not the government or the Armed Forces." (1/17/90)

1/17 At 10:30 am, the courthouse is surrounded by troops as soldiers and officers who did not present declarations yesterday are again brought under heavy guard; the press is prohibited from entering the premises, "under orders from above." The prosecuting attorneys are: Saul Zelaya, Eduardo Pineda, Alvaro Campos, Ricardo Zelaya, Jorge Figiac, Julio César Murcia, Sotero Consuett Diaz and Mario Umana. Defense attorneys are listed as José Oscar Caballero, Adafredo Salgado, Euligia Rodriguez and Raúl Mendez. Colonel Benavides is reportedly held at the National Guard, the others at the National Police. (DH 1/18, TV 6, 12 1/17)

1/17 No one has raised the issue but Attorney General Colorado assures the press that the extrajudicial confessions were obtained "without the use of torture." "They had physical examinations before they went to court . . . I have the impression that the material authors received orders . . . It is very difficult for a little soldier to say 'I'm going to kill so and so.' It is a delicate point." (TV 12)

1/18 "Salvadoran Attorney General Colorado announces that his office will act as the official prosecutor of the military personnel implicated in the murders of the Jesuits." (U.S. Embassy Report)

1/19 Vice-President Merino denies rumors of a coup. "This is totally false . . . The actions of the President are supported by the government and the Armed Forces, though, he admits, "some members of the army could be concerned about the detentions of their fellow officers." (TV 2)

1/19 Judge Zamora declares sufficient merit for the provisional detention of the nine accused. He sets an embargo of $8000 on the property of Colonel Benavides, approximately $3000 on each of the others. Arrest warrant is issued for the soldier who deserted in December. Defense attorneys expected to file appeals. (TV 6, 12) According to the formal charges, the assassinations were "planned and directed from the Military School" and the action was carried out by a commando unit formed for the special mission. Pvt. Oscar Mariano Amaya Grimaldi received the

AK47 used to execute the victims; another soldier was given the M16 for the "coup de grace." (DL 1/19)

1/19 "The judge announces that there is sufficient evidence to hold all eight prisoners under provisional arrest for the next stage in the judicial process." (U.S. Embassy Report)

1/19 Lieutenant Guevara Cerritos is accused of making the sign left on the gate, based on a handwriting analysis. (EM 1/19)

1/19 According to the declaration of Lt. Yusshy Mendoza, he received orders from Colonel Benavides on the night of the 15th to accompany the other two officers on an operation. Between 11:00 pm and 12:00 am he was called to Benavides' office and told, "You will accompany Espinosa on a mission." Lt. José Ricardo Espinosa Guerra said he received orders at 11:00 pm and was told by Benavides, "This is a situation in which it's them or us . . . We are going to begin with the leaders . . . Inside our sector we have the UCA and Ellacuría is there . . . You carry out the search . . . Your people know this place . . . Use the same plan as the day of the first search (November 13) . . . You have to eliminate him and I don't want any witnesses . . . Lt. Mendoza is going with you as head of the operation." Espinosa said, "This is a serious problem," and Benavides replied, "Don't worry, you have my support." Sgt. Tomás Zapata Castillo admitted he shot the two women while the others killed the priests. "I shot the women until I was sure they were dead so there wouldn't be any groaning." Corporal Angel Pérez Vasquez, Pvt. Oscar Mariano Amaya Grimaldi and Pvt. Jorge Alberto Sierra Ascencio allegedly killed the priests. The judge has 90-120 days to collect evidence and determine if the accused will face a jury trial or be released. (DH 1/20)

1/19 Jesuit Provincial José María Tojeira says, "the process is insufficient . . . We believe serious elements are missing, the intellectual authors . . . It is a little strange that one colonel would order a crime like this, more than anything because he (Benavides) is a circumspect man . . . Technically the investigation has been good . . . There is proof with ballistics tests against those who carried out the act." (TV 6)

1/19 Father Miguel Estrada, Rector of the UCA believes the investigation is "positive" but not concluded. "It lacks the intellectual authors . . . who must be punished." (YSU) "A real investigation that goes all the way to the intellectual authors would be a great gift to the Salvadoran people . . . peace with justice." (TV 12)

1/19 "The Judge acted in accordance with the law but now must investigate all the way to discover the intellectual authors," says María Julia Hérnandez. "This is an historic case which could demonstrate that justice can work in El Salvador." (Sonora)

1/20 Dr. Rubén Zamora says the investigation is "not finished. . . . One colonel could not have carried it out alone . . . and the problem is more fundamental than taking one colonel to court . . . There must be a real clean-up." (YSU, TV 12)

1/20 The declaration of Corporal Angel Pérez Vásquez is published by *Diario Latino*; Perez, a member of the 4th Company of the Atlacatl Battalion, says he received orders from Lt. Mendoza. He says he passed one body, then, "He grabbed my leg so I shot him four times." (DL 1/20)

1/22 Defense attorneys present an appeal, based on irregularities in the extrajudicial confessions. According to the law, even under the state of siege extrajudicial confessions must be taken within 72 hours of detention. Already eight days had passed. The accused were arrested on January 5, the declarations dated January 13. The attorneys also state that a lawyer should have been present during the process. "They are not 'clean' and have no merit," he says. Benavides should not be detained because he has denied the charges and the only evidence against him, aside from the declarations of the other accused, is that he was zone commander. The accused cannot testify against each other under Salvadoran law. The judge has three days to rule on the appeal. (TV 6, 12, EM, DL 1/22)

1/22 Defense attorneys file writ of habeas corpus demanding that the eight be released on the ground that the provisional detention order was improperly filed. The release of Colonel Benavides is demanded on the additional ground that he has been implicated by accomplices and under Salvadoran law the testimony of co-conspirators is inadmissible as evidence against other co-conspirators." (U.S. Embassy Report)

1/22 *Diario Latino* publishes declaration of Sgt. Tomás Zarpata Castillo, member of the 8th Company of the Atlacatl Battalion. Zarpata says he shot the women, "until I was sure they were dead and weren't groaning." (1/22/90)

1/24 Lt. Gonzalo Guevara Cerritos also accuses Benavides of giving the orders. (DL *1/24/90*)

1/24 Colonel Ponce denounces continuing speculation on the case, urging that anyone having proof should submit it to the judge, "or be quiet and stop trying to discredit the Armed Forces . . . This is dishonest, irresponsible and illegal." (EM 1/25)

1/25 Prosecuting attorneys oppose the defense appeal; in the case of Benavides the opinion of the prosecution is "sufficient circumstantial evidence" for provisional detention. (EM 1/25)

1/25 Declaration of Lt. José Ricardo Espinoza Guerra, company commander of the Atlacatl Battalion accuses Benavides of ordering "the elimination" of the Jesuits. (DL 1/25)

1/26 Roberto D'Aubuisson interviewed by the press for the first time in two months. He says he "laments" the assassinations but "it was an isolated action." "There is nothing more to investigate . . . It is not convenient to continue investigating the Armed Forces." (YSU)

1/26 President George Bush admits there is "some evidence" that Cristiani does not completely control the armed forces. (YSU)

1/26 Pvt. Oscar Mariona Amaya Grimaldi admits participating in the assassinations of three of the priests and of carrying the AK47. (*DL* 1/26/90)

1/27 In his testimony, Lt. Yusshy René Mendoza Vallecillos accuses Colonel Benavides of ordering the killings. (DL 1/27)

1/29 At 9:30 am, Judge Zamora announces his decision to deny the defense appeal; he also says a new witness, a woman, has been called to testify. (Sonora) He says the 72-hour time limit was not violated because the accused were not officially detained during the first days but were held under military arrest. The accused will not be transferred to prisons to await trial but will continue to be detained in various military installations. Zamora says he will call witnesses during the 90-to-120-day judicial investigation period. (TV 12)

1/29 Interviewed in Spain, Father Jon Sobrino says the investigation is creating "strong divisions" within the Armed Forces. (TV 12)

1/29 President Cristiani admits there are declarations but "no technical evidence" against Benavides. (LPG 1/29/90) He announces that all international investigators have left the country, "very pleased with the progress of the investigation." Colonel Avilés is not under arrest but is being interrogated . . . "His transfer to Washington has been suspended." (Sonora)

1/29 Colonel Mauricio Vargas says the investigation has caused "a lot of pain in the institution . . . , but building democracy is more important than an individual." (TV 12)

1/29 According to Colonel Ponce's declaration he ordered the formation of a "Security Command" to operate from the Military School under the responsibility of Benavides, beginning the afternoon of the 13th. (DL 1/29/90)

1/30 President Cristiani leaves for the U.S. saying he "cannot speculate on whether there will be further steps taken." (TV 6)

1/30 Jesuit Provincial José María Tojeira says the UCA will name a lawyer to represent the institution as the victim in the investigation and to demand indemnities for the physical destruction. (TV 6)

1/30 "The memory of the Jesuits deserves more than an investigation conducted only for the purpose of assuring U.S. aid," says Rubén Zamora. "They are only doing it for the aid and that is offensive to their memory . . . This case must establish a precedent so that it doesn't happen again." (TV 6) "It is positive that officers have been charged . . . but hardly likely that Benavides could have made this decision . . . The Director of the Military School does not have responsibility for troops much less an elite battalion like the Atlacatl . . . We don't agree with D'-

Aubuisson . . . His statement that the case is closed sounded like a cover-up." (Sonora)

1/30 *Diario Latino* begins publication of the Lawyers' Committee report on the witness, Lucia Barrera de Cerna. (1/30)

February 1990

2/1 Judge Zamora is interviewing an average of two witnesses a day; a defense attorney says the witnesses, soldiers, are presenting contradictory statements. "Some have said that their fellow soldiers never left the military barracks during that day." A total of 180-200 witnesses are scheduled to be interviewed. (LPG 2/2/90)

2/1 Cristiani gave "strong assurances" in Washington that the investigation will continue "even if it implicates more senior officers." (LAT 2/2/90)

2/4 *Miami Herald* (2/4) and *Washington Post* (2/6) publish stories on the deteriorating relations between the U.S. military advisors and the Salvadoran military stemming from the assassinations. According to the *Herald*, top military commanders held two meetings within hours of the massacre, one from 7:30-10:30 pm on the night of the 15th of November. Thirty commanders including Ponce, Bustillo and Benavides met to review the critical situation and decided on the use of aircraft, heavy artillery and armored battalions in the capital and on a plan to assassinate guerrilla leaders and destroy rebel command centers. The UCA was cited as a "launching point" for guerrilla operations. "This may have created the atmosphere that led Benavides to order the killings." Cristiani was called at 10:30 pm to authorize the use of airpower and artillery in the capitol. He gave his authorization.

At 8:00 am on the 16th, a meeting of intelligence officers in the building shared by the CIA and DNI (National Intelligence Center) was interrupted by a junior officer with news of the assassination of Ellacuría . . . " Everyone clapped" according to the *Herald,* and "cheered," according to the *Post.* Not until January 2 did U.S. advisor Major Eric Buckland, a close friend of Colonel Carlos Avilés, inform the Embassy that Benavides was being accused of ordering the operation. "The Salvadorans view the U.S. trainers as spies," says the *Post*. "If the deteriorating relations continue it could circumscribe U.S. influence and in the long run jeopardize U.S. willingness to provide military aid." (WP 2/6/90)

2/7 Colonel Ponce says Benavides and the seven others in custody remain on active duty, are receiving salaries and are in the custody of the National Police. (TV 6, 12)

2/8 Defense attorneys are "very concerned with the slowness of the Judge" in taking declarations from witnesses. The court has a list of 200 persons to interview. (LPG 2/8/90)

2/8 Forty-five members of the Atlacatl Battalion cited to testify have not appeared. (TV 12) A later report indicates the soldiers may be "brought by force" to present declarations. (Sonora)

2/8 During a Congressional hearing Bernard Aronson admits there was a meeting of high level officers on the night before the killings; Senator Thomas Harkin requests an investigation of that meeting. (TV 12)

2/9 Colonel Ponce rejects any link between the Armed Forces as an institution and the assassinations, saying that the meetings were "daily and routine beginning November 9th." "They are still trying to politicize the case . . . The work meeting cannot be related in any way to the case . . . Speculation that the Armed Forces as an institution are involved must be ended." (TV 12) "The speculations are a maneuver of the communists." (DH 2/10/90)

2/10 María Julia Hérnandez says, "Only part of the truth is known about the assassinations . . . It is impossible that one colonel could have ordered the operation." (YSU) The Jesuit massacre was "an act of weakness and panic . . . a military operation, not a death squad action." (DL 2/10/90)

2/11 Fifteen Congress members and their staff assistants arrive at 2:00 pm at Ilopango Airport. The delegation, led by Rep. Joe Moakley represents the Congressional Task Force on the assassinations established by Congress member Tom Foley. They are met by Ambassador Walker and other Embassy officials. Walker assures the press that the meeting of the High Command on November 15th was "routine." (TV 12)

2/12 The delegation visits the UCA to meet with Rector Miguel Estrada and Jesuit Provincial José María Tojeira. They visit the site of the massacre and place flowers on the tombs. Tojeira reconstructs the crime. (TV 12) Father Estrada says the UCA is "partially satisfied" with the investigation "but the problem is the intellectual authors ... The investigation is focusing on the material authors and that is not enough." (YSKL) Tojeira discusses the treatment of the witness in the U.S. saying he was "too naive" in trusting the Embassy to accompany her to Miami and turn her immediately over to the Jesuits. "I was very surprised to learn the FBI held her for eight days ... That was not our agreement." He also tells the delegation that 217 troops were in the area of the UCA on the night of the crime, 47 inside the campus. (Sonora)

2/12 The delegation meets for two hours with Colonels Ponce and Zepeda. Ponce later says, "We talked clearly and honestly about our position . . . The Armed Forces is open to investigation . . . Anyone who has evidence should present it . . . The Congress members know the progress of the Armed Forces . . . They know the criteria of the institution." (TV 12)

2/13 Congress members meet with President Cristiani for two hours, then with Archbishop Rivera y Damas, Bishop Rosa Chávez and María Julia Hérnandez. After the meeting in the Archdiocese Rosa Chávez says, "We believe military aid should be conditioned on human rights . . . and that the investigation must continue . . . It was not just the order from one colonel . . . There are things to discover, they have not investigated deeply enough." (TV 6, 12)

2/13 Delegation of rectors of Jesuit universities in the United States and members of the Lawyers' Committee for Human Rights arrives in the country. (TV 12)

2/14 Congressional delegation holds a press conference before departing the country. Joe Moakley reads the statement citing the objectives of the trip: .

1. To determine whether the investigation has led to the identification of all those responsible for the crime.

2. To ascertain whether it is likely that they will be brought to justice.

3. To gauge the overall climate of respect for human rights in El Salvador.

4. To assess prospects for an end to the war and a lasting peace.

The statement says that the investigation has been characterized by "good police work" but it is not over. "Important leads and allegations remain to be fully investigated . . . namely reports which suggest that the intellectual authors of the murders have not been identified and suggestions that there may have been a cover-up of this crime by some in the armed forces . . . We join with our Ambassador in insisting that these specific allegations must be thoroughly investigated."

"With respect to the next phase of the judicial process, we fear that presently available evidence may be insufficient to bring all the murderers to justice. We are deeply concerned about this prospect ... and strongly support current as well as possible new efforts by the United States to assist in every possible way the Salvadoran Government in its investigatory and judicial efforts."

"With respect to the overall climate of respect for human rights, we have strong concerns. First, we condemn . . . in the strongest possible terms . . . the FMLN offensive and the needless bloodshed that resulted. In prosecuting the offensive, the FMLN is guilty of serious violations of human rights and caused a serious setback to the prospects for a peaceful settlement to the war. "With regard to the Salvadoran armed forces . . . a central question for the task force is whether the human rights problem in El Salvador . . . including the Jesuit killings . . . are the actions of a few renegade military figures or whether, in fact, they stem from attitudes and actions that go to the very heart of the armed forces and other major institutions in this country. Encouraging genuine change in these institutions remains the greatest challenge facing El Salvador; a challenge that despite enormous investments of money and effort, has not yet been fully met. Given the tragedy of the Jesuit case, it is particularly important that the armed forces be able to distinguish as an institution between those who take up arms against the Government and those whose religious and political convictions simply place them at odds with the Government. Lastly, with respect to prospects for peace, we believe that the way to end the fighting is through negotiations. Both here in El Salvador and in the United States, the Congress is being urged by some to end military aid to El Salvador or to condition aid on peace negotiations between the Salvadoran Government and the FMLN. We strongly urge the opening of honest dialogue that can lead to an end to the fighting, and to peace with freedom and justice for all Salvadorans." (Statement 2/14/90)

2/14 ARENA Deputy Gloria Salguera Gross denounces the delegation as "intervening in internal affairs . . . The Democrats are only acting in their own interests . . . It is unjust to condition aid . . . and incorrect for five million Salvadorans to suffer because of one deplorable act." (TV 6)

2/14 The U.S. Jesuit delegation will meet with President Cristiani, Colonel Ponce, Judge Zamora, the Attorney General, the Supreme Court and the Special Investigations Unit. (TV 12)

2/15 President Cristiani says the Congressional visit was "positive" and adds, "There is no evidence to suggest the involvement of other military officers in the assassinations." (TV 12)

2/16 Ambassador Walker says the Congress members were "satisfied with their investigation. I am optimistic that the economic and military aid will not be cut . . . It is important that the truth comes out." (TV 12)

2/16 Four soldiers from the Atlacatl Battalion appear in court to give declarations after two citations were ignored. According to one of them, "The Colonel didn't know about it before but now we are ready." A defense attorney notes "irregularities and changes" in the statements. (TV 12)

2/16 Three months after the assassinations, a death squad, the "Grupo Anti-Communista Savadorena," "GAS," issues a communique "condemning to death" fifteen persons, among them seven already assassinated, including five of the Jesuits. Each person on the list is presented with an alleged pseudonym and political responsibility:

Ignacio Ellacuría: "Ricardo", International Political Commission

Ignacio Martín Baró: "José or Manuel", Commission of International Support

Segundo Montes: "Rafael or Samuel", Communications Commission

Juan Ramon Moreno: "Colocho", Medical Commission

Amando López: "Roberto", National Political Commission

(The name of Amando López is repeated and Joaquin López is omitted.)

Dr. Héctor Oquelí Colíndres, assassinated on January 12 is on the list as is FMLN commander Dimas Rodriguez, killed in combat on December 10.

The other eight names are of FMLN political and military leadership.

"Many of these criminal terrorists have already died and now can no longer harm our Salvadoran people who were victims of the genocide of November 11th last year." (DL 2/17/90).

2/19 Three more soldiers of the Atlacatl Battalion appear in court to present declarations; all say they were positioned in the "Torre Democracía" on the night of the killings and deny seeing any vehicles in the area "due to lack of visibility." (TV 6) Torre Democracía is the highest building in the country and looks down on the UCA; there was a full moon that night.

2/19 Fourteen of the fifty Atlacatl soldiers cited have presented declarations to date. (TV 12)

2/19 Seven Danish parliamentarians are in the country to study the situation in general and, in particular, progress on the Jesuit case. (TV 6)

2/21 Colonel Mauricio Vargas says the Armed Forces "is very sorry to see one of its members compromised . . . but we have turned him over to the courts." (DH 2/22)

2/22 *Washington Post* reports the Embassy is "uncomfortable" about the preferential treatment Colonel Benavides is receiving; he is said to be living in a luxury apartment inside the National Police Headquarters and is not confined . . . He has reportedly been seen at the elegant beach hotel owned by the Armed Forces. (WP/TV 12)

2/22 Rector of the UCA says the University has given up the idea of participating in the investigation. Miguel Estrada also confirms that the troops who are now presenting declarations to the court "are giving different testimonies than they did in their extrajudicial declarations." (TV 6)

2/23 Rubén Zamora says if the information published in the *Washington Post* is true "it points out a fundamental problem . . . The impunity that the Armed Forces enjoys must end." (TV 12)

2/28 Testifying before House Finance Committee, Secretary of State James Baker says the U.S. Government is "indignant" about the preferential treatment given to Colonel Benavides. "We are dealing with the Salvadoran Government on this." (TV 6)

March 1990

3/3 Judge Zamora says the case will not be moved to Santa Tecla as requested by the defense . . . "Only the Supreme Court can order a change of venue." (DL 3/3) According to a court employee, interviews of witnesses continue but "many" of the soldiers subpoenaed have not appeared and "there are no new elements" in the case. (EM 3/3)

3/4 Senator Edward Kennedy calls for a suspension of all aid to the country until human rights are respected and the Jesuit case resolved. (DH 3/5)

3/5 Four additional witnesses have presented declarations, all members of the National Police who were on duty in the area of the UCA November 15-16. They "had no additional information or evidence to offer," according to a defense attorney who says the case will be dismissed for lack of evidence. (TV 6)

3/7 Rumors circulate that Judge Zamora has been assassinated; dozens of reporters converge on the courthouse but the Judge is alive and well. He says he has not been pressured and has not requested security. "God will protect me." According to the radio report, lawyers involved in the case have requested salaries of $200,000 and guarantees of sanctuary in the U.S. if necessary. (YSU)

3/7 Press receives a death squad communiqué addressed to political parties, churches, unions, associations and diplomatic missions. The document, allegedly written on February 13 at a meeting of death squad members from all fourteen departments of the country, reads: "We are observing the crisis in the Armed Forces and in our beloved ARENA party . . . a crisis leading to vacillation and recognition of stupidities like human rights . . . and prosecution of members of the Armed Forces . . . The officers and troops charged in the Jesuit case must be released before Holy Week or we will take action against all persons in and out of the government involved in the case." The communique is signed by the General Command of the Death Squads, Aquiles Baires, Maximiliano Hérnandez Martinez and the Comite Pro-Salvacion. (Sonora 12:30 pm)

3/9 President Cristiani declares the death squads "have no reason to exist . . . We believe justice must flourish . . . This threat will not set back our efforts." (TV 6)

3/12 The threats are "absurd" says Colonel Ochóa Pérez. "The government will not submit to this blackmail." (DL) The threats "are an attempt to discredit the Armed Forces." (TV 12)

3/16 Human Rights Commission says the amnesty proposed in the Assembly for members of the military is "unjustifiable" if it includes the San Sebastian or Jesuit massacres. PDC leader Roberto Viera insists any amnesty "must not include the Jesuit case . . . That would be a grave error . . . The case is important for the political life of the country . . . for peace and justice." (EM)

3/20 Of 200 witnesses in the case, 75 have been interviewed, including soldiers, neighbors and UCA security guards; no new evidence has been provided according to court officials. (LPG)

3/21 Auxiliary Bishop Rosa Chávez has sent his declaration to Judge Zamora as requested by the Attorney General's office. (TV 12)

3/22 Defense formally presents petition requesting change of venue, arguing that the UCA is in the legal jurisdiction of the Santa Tecla court.

Defense attorney Mendez says the Judge should declare himself un-
qualified and withdraw from the case; he has 24 hours to rule on the
petition. (TV 12)

3/24 Interviewed by the *Washington Post*, Cristiani says he doubts
Colonel Benavides will be prosecuted and says he feels "frustrated" that
the Colonel is living in a luxury cell "but the Armed Forces have their
rules." (TV 12/WP)

3/25 "Segundo Montes" City inaugurated in Meanguera, Morazán.
(DL)

3/26 Jesuit Provincial José María Tojeira says it is "not believable"
that only Benavides gave the orders. "There are more people implicated . . . There was a group of high military officers who promised to
support him." According to Tojeira, Benavides' official diary notes a
"guerrilla attack" against the Theology Building of the UCA at 12:30 am
on the night of the massacre, two hours before the events occurred. (TV
12)

April 1990

4/4 Colonel Ponce denies that Benavides has ever left the jurisdiction of the Fourth Criminal Court and says the military "is not taking a position" on the case . . . The institution "has initiated a rigorous clean-up of troops and paramilitary . . . It is the permanent moral responsibility of the institution to remove elements that commit abuses." (EM)

4/4 Associated Press reports the White House is "hardening its attitude" toward El Salvador as a result of "difficulties" with Congress, especially "liberals" concerned about the Jesuit case. Aid could be conditioned on a resolution of the murders, overhaul of the legal system and a cleansing of the Armed Forces. (EM/AP)

4/17 José María Tojeira says defense attorneys are still attempting to move the case to Santa Tecla. "It's political," he says. "The move could be beneficial to the accused . . . with less press coverage and different judges." (TV 6)

4/18 Attorney General insists on the change of venue. "The appropriate judge is in the jurisdiction." (TV 6)

4/22 In the U.S., CBS program "Sixty Minutes" features a segment on the case. Retired Colonel Sigifredo Ochóa Pérez says he does not believe Col. Benavides planned the assassinations. "No, I don't think so. Knowing him, he is not a man who could make or conceive of a move as big as this. Benavides acted under orders. He didn't act alone."

Ed Bradley: "The Army says he misunderstood the orders, do you believe this?"

Ochóa Pérez: "No, I think it was all planned beforehand."

Bradley: "He had help from other senior officers in the Salvadoran military?"

Ochóa: "Yes."

Bradley: "And they planned the murders?"

Ochóa: "I believe so, yes." (TV 12/CBS)

(later)

Ochóa: "A group of commanders stayed behind (after the meeting on the night of the 15th). It seems each was responsible for a zone in San Salvador. They gave an order to kill leftists, just as Benavides did. I'll say it again. Benavides obeyed, it wasn't his decision."

Bradley says no other top commanders have been investigated and specifically refers to Colonel Zépeda. "Just five months before the murder of the Jesuits, according to a State Department document, Zépeda claimed the Jesuits . . . were planning guerrilla strategy. According to that same State Department document Zépeda probably was one of the officers to whom Benavides reported." Bradley also says, "It stunned us to find out that the American Embassy had given Colonel Ponce an audio tape of our interview with Ambassador Walker to help him prepare for us. So Ponce knew the questions we were likely to ask. Is the U.S. Embassy in cahoots with the army of El Salvador?" Several Jesuits, Lucia Cerna, Ambassador Walker and Congress member George Miller are also interviewed. The segment closes with an earlier interview of Martín Baró: "There is some environment of the possibility of being killed any moment of the day and the possibility of being involved in a violent clash at any moment. And you have to count on that." (CBS)

4/23 Channel 12 News plays the segment featuring Ochóa Pérez. (TV 12)

4/24 State Department declines to comment on questions raised by "Sixty Minutes" surrounding the conduct of Ambassador Walker. The Council of Hemispheric Affairs demands Walker be called before Congress to explain his actions, saying the Moakley Report "will not be complete without an interview with Walker." (EM/AP)

4/24 "We are evaluating what he said," Minister of Defense Larios responds to Ochóa's charges. "The case is in the courts and anyone who has additional information should present it . . . This does not affect the Armed Forces . . . The case is under the responsibility of the civilian authorities." (TV 12)

4/24 "The statements were very daring," says Deputy Julio Adolfo Rey Prendes. "Colonel Ochóa has a reputation for being very spontaneous . . . He could have problems explaining what he said." (TV 12)

4/25 *Boston Globe* and *Herald* reveal that the military personnel accused in the case were all trained either in the U.S. or by North American soldiers in El Salvador, with the exception of Benavides. (TV 12) Four were trained in Georgia and North Carolina, four by U.S. trainers in the country. The information was provided to Moakley by Carl Ford, Assistant Secretary of Defense for International Affairs. (DL)

4/25 "Unidentified military officer" accuses Ochóa of "damaging the image of the army and the country . . . endangering military aid . . . and supporting the international left." (DH)

4/25 *Diario Latino* publishes entire transcript of "Sixty Minutes."

4/25 Colonel Ochóa releases a statement in response to criticisms: "The attitude of some bad elements of the Armed Forces must not be allowed to be used against the Institution . . . It is proper to cleanse the ranks . . . In proposing this necessary clean-up I am responding to a historical necessity . . . It is not the person who points out the evil who is creating the damage but the one who acts against humanitarian principles. . . . When I referred to those who executed the order to assassinate the Jesuits, they were doing this: complying with orders . . . I haven't done anything more than say publicly what the people say and express in whispers . . . It is assumed that some information exists and that it is in the hands of certain sectors who for one reason or another have not provided that information to the corresponding authorities." (EM 4/26)

4/25 House Foreign Affairs Committee votes to support a 50% cut in aid and a total cut if the government does not conduct a broad investigation of the case and carry out serious negotiations. (TV 6)

4/25 Judge Zamora rejects the petition of the Attorney General for a change of venue and requests the Treasury Police to remit two of the accused for interviews, Gonzalo Guevara Cerritos and José Ricardo Espinoza Guerra. (LPG)

4/25 The Judge's ruling states that according to the National Geographic Institute, the Military School lies within the jurisdiction of San Salvador. (TV 12) The ruling also charges the nine accused with "crimes against the public order" and theft of $5000 (the award money presented to Ellacuría in Spain, just before he returned to El Salvador.) Members of the Honor Commission, named by President Cristiani early in January to determine the existence of sufficient evidence against the accused to prosecute the case, are subpoenaed to appear before the Judge, a legal move that reportedly "surprises" the defense. (DL, DH)

4/25 Members of the Honor Commission, previously unknown, are: Colonel Juan Vicente Equizabal Figueroa, Major José Roberto Zamora Hérnandez, Captain Juan Manuel Grijalva Torres, Rodolfo Parker (civilian), Antonio Augusto Gomez Zarate (civilian), General Rafael Villamariona (Air Force) and Colonel Israel Machuca (National Police), also members of the Commission will be permitted to submit notarized written statements. All will be asked to explain the evidence which led them to accuse Benavides. (LPG 4/26)

4/25 Colonel Carlos Avilés is back on active duty in the High Command, responsible for Psychological Operations. (TV 12)

4/25 In Washington, Arms Control and Foreign Policy Caucus issues a Staff Memorandum on the Atlacatl Battalion; the report charges the Battalion with responsibility for four massacres and six other specific cases since its founding in 1981. (Report)

4/26 President Cristiani says Ochóa's statements are not important . . . "Speculations don't help . . . to the contrary they obstruct the legal process." (TV 12)

4/26 Attorney General Colorado will ask Judge Zamora to subpoena Ochóa. (TV 12)

4/27 "Because of the Jesuit case many members of Congress believe there has been no progress on human rights," says Cristiani. "This is a mistaken perception . . . It is part of the FMLN strategy to weaken the Armed Forces." (DH 4/288)

4/30 Moakley Report released in Washington. The Task Force concludes that the investigation is "at a standstill" with "little possibility of justice . . . The lack of a continuous process together with certain aspects of Salvadoran law make it unlikely that justice will be served." The failure is "symptomatic of profound institutional problems in the exercise of justice." The report suggests Colonel Benavides would never have been arrested if a U.S. officer had not informed the Embassy of his involvement. Task Force members say they are "disillusioned" by the failure of the investigation unit and the judge to pursue the case but congratulate Cristiani for his "sincere effort." (EM 4/1)

4/30 In Washington, Ambassador Salaverria criticizes the "paternalistic" attitude of Congress saying, "We have our own convictions and only the judge can respond to this case. It is in his hands." (TV 6)

4/30 Ambassador Walker says he is concerned with the investigation and shares the opinion that "not much has been done. . . .They must work day and night . . . Judge Zamora has to do more . . . There are others in the military who must be subpoenaed . . . Ochóa, for example, believes there are others involved . . . The greatest weakness here is the administration of justice . . . Everyone agrees many changes are necessary . . . There is not enough pressure from the political parties . . . " (TV 6)

4/30 Defense attorneys present another appeal for change of venue, saying the judge's denial was "based on international law, not applicable here." (TV 6) No crime was committed in the Military School, according to the attorneys, and the UCA is located in the jurisdiction of Santa Tecla. (TV 6)

May 1990

5/1 Armed Forces publishes statement "emphatically and energetically" rejecting the charges of retired Colonel Ochóa Pérez as "irresponsible and biased . . . an effort to sow confusion and mistrust . . . to involve senior members of the High Command in the Jesuit case . . . We demand that Colonel Ochóa and anyone else who has information present it to the corresponding courts and not try to gain political points based on alleged charges that add to the scheme of disinformation which is being developed in a systematic way by the marxist leninist terrorists, both nationally and internationally . . . We condemn these irresponsible statements as an effort to undermine the institutionality of the state . . . only favoring the dark and nefarious interests of the enemies of democracy." (TV 6, 12, LPG, DH)

5/1 Secretary of State James Baker testifies before Senate Appropriations Committee; says aid could be cut. "Our assistance will be affected by the form in which this case is conducted . . . The Salvadoran Government understands this." (EM)

5/1 Captain José Alfonso Chávez Garcia of the Treasury Police, killed in action today in the capitol, was mentioned in the "Young Officers' Letter" in December as responsible for the murders along with Colonel Héctor Heriberto Hérnandez. (Letter)

5/1-2 FMLN conducts "mini-offensive" in the capitol and six departments "as a response to the impunity of the Armed Forces in human rights," including the "standstill and coverup" in the Jesuit case. (Sonora)

5/2 Colonel Ochóa releases a statement defending his position; says his objective is "justice . . . not to blame anyone . . . I am not the one responsible for any cut in military aid." (TV 12)

5/2 Ochóa's statement reads: "As a Deputy I have the right to express what I feel and, equally, as a citizen and as a military man my duty is to the Armed Forces . . . I accompanied the soldiers and never thought of personal enrichment when I was on active duty, as has occurred with other officers, though certainly not all. As a soldier I am concerned about the situation of the Armed Forces . . . I have never mentioned names and have only demanded justice . . . I can't accept that a decision of this nature came from one person acting alone and I believe there is a conspiracy against the Institution. The field officers, who fight every day, are worthy of praise but I must be critical of those who have taken advantage of the Institution and then shout to the heavens as if I were the one undermining the institutionality of the state . . . The case must be investigated fully ... They shouldn't be making ridiculous demands and looking for a confrontation with me . . . I don't want it . . . I'm not against anyone in particular." Ochóa says he knows who was in the meeting (when the Armed Forces document denouncing him was written) "and even who said that President Cristiani must remove me from CEL . . . I have the responsibility given to me by the President and I will stay as long as he wishes." (EM)

5/2 "Young Officers' Letter" released to the press supporting Colonel Ochóa's charges, expressing "sadness and indignation" at the situation of the Institution and the repercussions of the acts of a "small group of corrupt officers." In reference to the Jesuit case, the letter, signed by "Young Officers, Domingo Monterrosa Lives," says the officers intuitively knew what had occurred when they heard the news but thought the repercussions would be minimal "because the priests were militants of the FMLN" ; nevertheless, "we judged it to be an irrational and senseless act because it is one thing to fight openly against the terrorists but quite another to fight against the ideologues."

"The Commander-in-Chief of the Armed Forces (Cristiani) doesn't know the activities of the High Command, and in this case, from the beginning, a great deal of information has been kept classified from the President . . . One of our classmates implicated in the case was threatened that he would be accused of being a member of the FMLN unless he complied with the superior order . . . It must be on record in his declaration . . . The pressures against the implicated young officers have continued while the superior officer is peaceful in his detention, with many comforts for which Colonel Carrillo, one of those who from the beginning, along with Colonels Ponce and Montano, opposed [the arrests], is responsible."

The letter points out two cases of "betrayal" by the U.S. Embassy, the first involving Colonel Carlos Avilés Buitrago "who on his own account investigated the extenuating circumstances of the case and in an informal way, gave the clue of those responsible. Then the recent case of the CBS program where Ambassador Walker alerted the High Command of information about the case . . . "

On the possible aid cuts and Colonel Ochóa, the letter continues: "They are trying to blame an ex-officer and commander as responsible for discrediting the institution . . . because of his statements on CBS . . . Is it a secret that Colonel Benavides' superior officer in all his operations and under the rules of our institution is Colonel Zépeda, then the Minister of Defense? The question is: who besides Colonel Benavides was involved in the operation, who was in the meetings at 3:00 and 5:00 pm in the office of Colonel Zépeda, not only Colonel Benavides but also other officers of the lowest graduation class. "The Ochóa case must be given more attention ... He has said what many of us cannot express because we would be sanctioned . . . Beginning May 1st we will be attentive to the events surrounding the Ochóa and Jesuit cases, which must result in an end to protectionism of superior officers who commit abuses, issuing orders that are violations of the laws of our country." The letter names "the group" of corrupt officers as Ponce, Montano, Fuentes, Carrillo, Rubio, Majano Araugo, Hérnandez, Staben and Zépeda . . . "The weight of the law must fall on them in this case . . . " (DL 5/4/90)

5/2 Judge Zamora issues a statement saying the Moakley Report will be included in the official records of the case. Zamora will subpoena Colonel Carlos Avilés and "possibly the U.S. advisor." A member of the Honor Commission, subpoenaed last week, does not appear today as scheduled. (TV 12) Government Secretary of Information, Mauricio Sandoval, says the case will go to trial in 90 days. (LPG 5/3)

5/3 President Cristiani says the Letter "lacks any credibility." (TV 12)

5/3 Channel 12 television news "apologizes" for reading portions of the Letter last night, saying it was "an error" . . . "The letter came to us anonymously . . . We offer our most sincere apologies and hope that this will not be misinterpreted." (TV 12)

5/3 High Command "emphatically rejects" the authenticity of the Letter and says it is "grey propaganda" . . . "There is no person or group of persons who take responsibility for the publication of this statement which has propagandistic tendencies that support the FMLN . . . " (TV 12, DH 5/4)

5/4 Bernard Aronson is interviewed on satellite television by Salvadoran journalists. He acknowledges "frustration" in Washington about the case but confirms continued support of the Cristiani Government. Aronson says the case was "a terrible and inexcusable crime . . . There have been too many crimes like this during the past ten years and it seems that no one has been punished . . . The case is the 'test of fire' for the government . . . It is encouraging that the accused will be tried in 90 days as President Cristiani announced, but there are certain aspects of Salvadoran law that make it difficult to find someone guilty of a conspiracy . . . We don't understand why this exists and why the Assembly doesn't change it, but this cannot be an excuse." (LPG)

5/4 Judge Zamora issues a press release on "progress" in the investigation. He reports that the registration book from the Military School containing information on the night of November 15-16 has been "mislaid." Two members of the Honor Commission subpoenaed to appear in court (Dr. Antonio Augusto Gomez Zarate and Rodolfo Parker Soto) did not appear. Four cadets who were on guard duty in the Military School the night of the crime are "out of the country" and unavailable to present declarations; three of them are "studying" in the U.S., the fourth in Panama. The three in the U.S. are César Moises Rivera Pérez, Raúl Galan Hérnandez and Wilfredo Aguilar Alvarado. Erick Othmaro Granados Moran is said to be in Panama. (TV 12, LPG) *Diario De Hoy* says the "loss" of the registration book will "impede the investigation of the case . . . which is being exploited by the left and other sectors." (5/4)

5/4 Vice-Minister of Public Security, Colonel Montano, says Col. Ochóa "may have some followers" in the institution, "but not many. He has a heroic but also negative record." The Letter, he says, "has no credibility . . . It could be from the left or perhaps from someone who is out of the Armed Forces and wants to return." (TV 6)

5/5 Colonel Zépeda says he wants to present a declaration to the judge "because of media reports that involve him." (LPG)

5/5 A "source" in the Attorney General's office says the case will go to trial soon, "since the witnesses who have not given statements are not responding to the subpoenas." (EM)

5/5 The loss of the registration book is "unusual," says María Julia Hérnandez, and an example of the "lack of will to prosecute the case . . . We are very concerned that the case is not advancing as it should be . . . Colonel Ochóa's statements confirm what we have said from the beginning . . . Ochóa is a military man, he knows the institution very well." (TV 12)

5/5 The disappeared book "is a problem for the courts," says Colonel Ponce, and the situation of the four cadets outside the country is "normal," according to the Chief of Staff who says they have been away since January. (TV 12)

5/6 Auxiliary Bishop Rosa Chávez calls on the military to "examine its conscience . . . to discover errors which have contributed to the war." The Letter, "whether or not it is authentic" . . . "raises issues which must be examined." (TV 12)

5/7 *New York Times* says recent setbacks in the case, including the loss of crucial evidence, "make it more difficult to investigate other senior officers" . . . "The obstructions could bring the U.S. Congress to cut aid." According to the *Times,* not only the registration book is missing, but also Benavides' personal diary. (Sonora)

5/7 Ochóa's statements were "foolhardy," says Colonel Zépeda, and "a danger to the High Command of the Armed Forces." The Colonel says his name "has been mentioned" in relation to the case but he has never been asked to testify. (DH)

5/7 The charges are "absurd," says Zépeda. "I was one of the first to be interested in investigating the case . . . It is absurd that they are trying to involve me . . . We have adversaries, enemies in this conflict . . . I totally reject the charges . . . Everyone knows the Vice-Minister does not have direct relations with troops . . . My responsibility is administrative and advisory . . . I didn't have any relation to Benavides or the Military School except on administrative issues." Zépeda says the objective of the "Sixty Minutes" segment was "to support a cut in aid" and informs the press that he has sent a note of protest to CBS for implying he was involved in the assassinations. (TV 12)

5/7 President Cristiani insists the "disappearance" of the log book and Benavides' diary "must be investigated" and the four missing cadets "must be called to testify." (EM) "What's the difference if they come from Suchitoto or the United States to testify?" (YSU)

5/7 Minister of Defense Larios assures the press he knows nothing about the missing books and says the cadets "will return the moment they are called . . . It's all completely normal." (TV 6, 12)

5/7 In a press statement, Judge Zamora says the case is not ready to go to trial; it is still in the preliminary phase . . . "There are witnesses to be interviewed . . . It cannot be done precipitously." (Sonora)

5/7 Zamora has a long meeting with Embassy officials. (EM/AP)

5/8 Supreme Court rejects charges of the Moakley Commission that the case is at a standstill . . . "The careless and irresponsible charges that the case is held up are false." (EM)

5/8 *Washington Post* says the case is "paralyzed." (Sonora)

5/8 The possible promotion of Colonel Ponce to Minister of Defense and the retirement of Colonel Zépeda "could seriously affect the negotiations," according to a statement from the FMLN General Command, by "breaking the chain of responsibility for the Jesuit assassinations." (DL)

5/8 A legal source tells Associated Press that the case "could go to trial at the end of the year," and, "there is little possibility Benavides will be convicted." If the Judge works hard, he says, "and there are no problems," it could happen by the end of 1990. Benavides apparently mentioned the diary in his extrajudicial declaration but later denied its existence in his judicial statement . . . "The court has never seen the diary." (EM/AP)

5/8 State Department spokesperson Richard Boucher reports that the Department has asked the Embassy to confirm the disappearance of evidence and warns that the loss "endangers the efforts to broaden the investigation and could have an impact on the prosecution of those who are implicated." He says the four cadets are on "routine" study tours and will return to El Salvador on May 24th . . . "Salvadoran authorities have offered to bring them back sooner if necessary." Boucher says the U.S. has been "assured" by Cristiani that all the "clues" will be investigated and the process "resumed." Asked when it was "interrupted," he says he "doesn't know." He concludes, "The U.S. hopes that Cristiani, the judicial system and the Armed Forces comply with promises to investigate in depth the case that has created a strong sentiment in Congress supporting a cut in aid." (DL)

5/8 White House spokesperson Marlin Fitzwater reports that President Cristiani met last night with White House advisor John Sununu in Costa Rica "at the request of President Cristiani." Sununu warned Cristiani that the Jesuit investigation "is a serious matter for the U.S.," and that the trial "will have a significant impact . . . Opposition to aid is increasing due to the Moakley Report." Fitzwater says Cristiani is "proceeding energetically" and the U.S. "has taken his word." (Sonora) This is the first time a high level U.S. official has publicly made the connection between the case and continued aid. (DL)

5/8 *Diario Latino* begins publication of the Moakley Report; *Proceso* (publication of the UCA) publishes entire document.

5/8 Judge Zamora subpoenas two of the cadets from the Military School, José Wilfredo Aguilar Alvarado (Fort Benning) and Erick Otmaro Granados Moran (in Panama). (Sonora) Subpoenas are also issued for two members of the Honor Commission, Major José Roberto Zamora Hérnandez and Captain Juan Manuel Grijalva Torres; second subpoenas are issued to the two civilian members who failed to appear last week, Rodolfo Parker and Antonio Augusto Gomez Zarate. (TV 12)

5/9 *Washington Post* publishes first interview with Colonel Benavides, conducted by Evans and Novak. The article, entitled "Jesuit

Assassinations . . . Who Gave the Order?", says Benavides was "calm" throughout the 2-hour-20-minute interview and responded "without hesitation" to questions. He denied having ordered the three lieutenants to assassinate the Jesuits and says he was "surprised" when he learned of the events; he "believed it was the work of the guerrillas." He was "surprised" again on January 6th when he was presented with the letter written by a U.S. officer (Major Buckland) stating that Colonel Avilés had informed him that Benavides ordered the assassinations. Avilés told Benavides he never made the accusation, "but the letter prevailed" after the testimonies of Yusshy Mendoza, José Espinoza and Gonzalo Cerritos. "Benavides does not believe the lieutenants acted on their own accord, nor does he believe there is a conspiracy in the army against him . . . If he was lying, he is a first-rate artist . . . The statements appear to be of a simple man, calm and without imagination." Benavides suggested that the three lieutenants will withdraw their accusations against him. (DL/WP)

5/9 Colonel Montano says he agrees with the *Post* . . . "In my personal opinion, I believe Benavides is innocent and that he was hit hard by the deaths of the Jesuits . . . He has been condemned without a trial . . . I was present when he was told that he would be detained . . . He collaborated and made himself available for the investigation . . . I noted that he received the news that he would have to make a declaration with a great deal of surprise and categorically denied his participation." (LPG 5/10) "Supposedly they are looking for someone high in the Armed Forces," he says, but "you can't blame the owners of a factory for the mistakes of the workers." (TV 6)

5/9 Judge Zamora receives a copy of the Moakley Report in Spanish; issues second subpoenas for Lt. Col. Juan Vicente Equizabal and Major Roberto Zamora. (DL) Attorney General's office presents second formal petition for change of venue . . . (DH 5/10)

5/10 "The only person who can determine the guilt or innocence of Colonel Benavides is the judge," says Cristiani, calling for an end to speculation on the case from everyone "including members of the government. We have freedom of expression here but these statements only impede the investigation . . . We will continue our policy of not expressing any opinions on his guilt or innocence." (TV 12) The President also says the Moakley Report is "biased." "The case is not at a standstill . . .

The Report contains many speculations which are sometimes treated as facts . . . This impedes the legal process." The Report "is only a report on the current situation . . . The final report will come at the end of the legal process." (TV 12)

5/10 Asked about his meeting with Presidential Advisor John Sununu, the President responds, "He made it clear that the assassination of the Jesuits was in the atmosphere, especially at the level of the Congress and Senate and that they are waiting for the development of the legal process . . . I explained what is happening now and what is to follow . . . I also informed him of the speculations that are occurring." (LPG 5/11)

5/10 The President has ordered a full investigation of the missing books and says the cadets have either returned to the country or will be here today to present declarations. (DL)

5/10 Defense attorneys denounce "foreign pressure . . . directing the course of the case." Attorney Carlos Méndez says Judge Zamora "is showing that he does not have autonomy . . . It is no secret that he meets with people from the U.S. to analyze the case." Legal assistant for the defense, Eulogio Barahona also deplores the "North American intervention," saying, "It is as though Salvadorans pressured the United States to tell us finally who killed Kennedy." Mendez says Benavides is an officer with a clean service record, of "irreproachable conduct." And, "They made a public scandal about the absence of the four cadets, but all third year cadets are sent to continue their weapons study in the exterior." (EM)

5/10 Colonel Elena Fuentes denounces the "international campaign to discredit the military institution . . . which for ten years has protected our right to enjoy the democracy we have now." (TV 6)

5/11 Two of the cadets, José Wilfredo Aguilar Alvarado and Erick Otmoro Granados Moran, testify today from 9:00 am - 1:00 pm. According to a court source they deny having been on duty in the Military School the night of November 15-16, "which contradicts the investigation commission . . . Either they are lying or the commission is lying," says the reporter. (TV 12)

5/11 The Supreme Court is not "violating the autonomy" of Judge Zamora by releasing his reports as court communiqués. (LPG)

5/12 Noted jurist Francisco Lima says the investigation is opening up "little by little" due to pressure from the U.S. (TV 12)

5/14 In Paris, Archbishop Rivera y Damas reveals that he and Bishop Gregorio Rosa Chávez were on a list of persons to be "eliminated" on the night of November 15-16, along with other persons who denounce human rights violations. He says both he and the Bishop have "repeatedly" received death threats. (TV 12)

5/14 The two civilian members of the Honor Commission, Rodolfo Parker Soto and Dr. Antonio Augusto Gomez Zarate appear in court today after receiving second subpoenas. They deny that the Commission interrogated the accused in January. Court sources say Colonel Machuca presented his written sworn testimony to the court on May 11. (TV 12)

5/14 According to the testimonies of the civilian members of the Honor Commission, the Commission worked from January 5-12 but did not interrogate anyone, "only exhorted everyone to tell the truth." The Commission visited the UCA "to be certain of the events" but did not conduct an investigation and did not elaborate a written report of their work. Colonel Machuca's written testimony was received last week but General Villamariona has yet to submit a statement. (TV 12) In Colonel Machuca's statement he reportedly says the Commission "only reviewed documentation." (YSU)

5/15 Cadets César Moises Rivera Pérez and Raúl Galan Hérnandez appear in court today to present testimonies; no information available on their statements. (TV 6, 12)

5/15 José María Tojeira expresses the dissatisfaction of the Jesuits with the progress of the case and says he disagrees with Benavides' declaration of innocence . . . "There is sufficient proof to involve him . . . He wrote false information in his diary and made no effort to investigate . . . I believe Colonel Montano must provide evidence and promote a serious investigation . . . We maintain our theory that it was not only Benavides but someone with more power." "The investigation stopped in January," he continues . . . "They said, 'that is as far as it goes' . . . The Special Investigation Unit has stopped its work . . . This situation reflects the interests of someone that the investigation go no further." (TV 6) "There is no willingness to go further with the case . . . The missing books, the problem of the cadets, the behavior of the Honor Commission . . . demonstrate that someone is trying to prevent any progress . . . They are attempting to blame the judicial system, which has made mistakes, but more powerful forces are responsible . . . Without further pressure from the U.S., the case will be forgotten." (TV 12)

5/15 A third communiqué from "Young Officers" is dated May 15 and released May 17. The letter accuses Colonels Ponce, Zépeda and Montano and General Larios, "supported by other commanders," of blocking the investigation and of ordering the execution of Captain Alfonso Chávez Garcia, the Treasury Police officer, accused in the first "Young Officers Letter," of leading the operation against the Jesuits. According to the communiqué, Chávez did not die in combat on May 1st but was killed by a special forces team "as part of a plan to erase all clues that can lead to those truly responsible and at the same time to exonerate the officers who have been falsely involved." The letter calls for the immediate resignation of the hierarchy. (Letter)

5/16 Six months since the Jesuit assassinations. Minister of Defense Larios sends a letter to Judge Zamora expressing the "firm" support of the Armed Forces in efforts to "clear up" the case and willingness of the institution to "cooperate" in facilitating declarations of any member of the military or civilian who works for the institution. (LPG 5/16) He asks that all documentation or requests referring to the case be sent directly to him. (EM)

5/16 Colonel Ochóa Pérez has been subpoenaed to appear in Judge Zamora's court. (DL)

5/16 Although prosecutors and some members of the Honor Commission have stated that the Commission did not write a report, President Cristiani says he has the report "and will turn it over to the Judge if it is requested." (DH 5/17)

5/16 Statement issued from the Supreme Court says all four cadets denied the information from the Special Investigations Unit that they were on duty the night of the assassinations. (YSU)

5/16 Supreme Court President Dr. Mauricio Gutierrez Castro, in Spain for a seminar, assures the press that the Court wants the case resolved. "The process is continuing honestly and rapidly," he says, but "excessive pressure can prejudice the case." (DH)

5/16 "How are the police going to continue looking for evidence if their boss (Colonel Montano) says the accused are innocent?" asks Rubén Zamora. (TV 12)

5/16 Demonstrations reported in the U.S. on the six-month anniversary of the assassinations; 500 North Americans and Salvadorans block the Federal Building in Los Angeles; 300 block the entrance to the Salvadoran Consul in L.A.; demonstrations also reported in New York, Washington, San Francisco and Houston. All protest the assassinations and demand an end to military aid. (Sonora)

5/17 Press receives "Communiqué #3" from the "Young Officers Command," accompanied by a note saying, "as you understand for obvious reasons we cannot provide our names," requesting publication. Radio Sonora says it cannot be read because it is anonymous; the letter is not mentioned on the television news but is published in *Diario Latino* and quickly distributed around the capital, hand to hand. The letter accuses the military hierarchy of ordering the execution of Captain Alfonso Chávez Garcia.

"The Young Officers Command denounces and accuses the military hierarchy of the Armed Forces, composed of Colonels Ponce, Zépeda and Montano and General Larios, supported by other military commanders, of setting in action a plan to block the investigation regarding the true assassins of the Jesuit priests. Through our intelligence sources we have proven that within this plan is the physical elimination of some officers that are linked to or know something about the case. This is how Captain Alfonso Chávez Garcia, officer of the Treasury Police (was killed.) We pointed him out in our first communiqué in November as the leader of the operation, ordered by Col. Héctor Heriberto Hérnandez. It is false that Captain Chávez died in combat (on May 1st). He fell in a trap set by the military hierarchy. Two members of the special forces eliminated him so that it appeared as though he was killed in combat with the terrorists. This is a plan to erase all the clues that can lead to those truly responsible and at the same time to exonerate the officers who have been falsely involved, as scapegoats."

"In the face of these serious events, the Young Officers Command expresses profound indignation and demands the resignation of the military hierarchy so they do not continue creating divisions, revulsion and dishonor within our institution. They have fallen so low that they have no moral right to wear the honorable military uniform. They are doing more damage to the Armed Forces than the terrorists themselves. To our fellow young officers, we call on you to unite with our movement of salvation of the Armed Forces, to incorporate for the rescue and cleansing of the ranks to return the [institution] to its true nature and to the mission for which it was created."

"Remember, officer, that when the superior is wrong, the subaltern has the legitimate right to insubordination. The current command hierarchy has lost all moral right to command, to be conspiring against members of the same institution with the vile purpose of covering up the bad elements that are doing such damage. For the honor of the Armed Forces." May 15, San Salvador. (Communiqué)

5/17 Colonel Montano dismisses the communiqué as "lacking any credibility." He also affirms that a cut in aid "will be negative for the country and the institution," but, "We are Salvadorans and with or without the aid we will continue the struggle. We are convinced the Government will go all the way to end the war." (TV 6)

5/17 The Dean of the Economic School of the UCA, Dr. Francisco Javier Ibizate, says the Jesuit investigation "is static due to lack of witnesses. The judge is wearing lead boots, but he is doing what he can under the circumstances." (EM) "It is not Zamora's fault," says Ibizate. "We agree with what he is trying to do. The cadets denied they were on duty or 'didn't remember'. All these obstacles are creating great difficulties for the judge." (TV 6)

5/18 In the Jesuit case, Judge Zamora rules the change of venue petition "without merit." He asks the Special Investigation Unit (SIU) to explain to him next week the evidence on which they determined the names of the four cadets supposedly on duty in the Military School on the night of the murders. He also requests Colonel Ricardo Casanova Sandoval, current Director of the Military School to inform the court as to the whereabouts of the missing log book and who was on duty that night. Zamora announces he will subpoena two of the members of the Honor Commission for the second time, the Lt. Colonel and the Major. (Sonora)

5/19 The Jesuit investigation is "going well," according to the President, who says a new report will be issued next week. He mentions the letter from the Minister of Defense to the Judge as an effort to facilitate the process. (TV 12)

5/19 Colonel Sigifredo Ochóa Pérez sends a written declaration to Judge Zamora. He says he will not discuss the contents, "secrecy responds to the legal procedures. It is up to the Judge," but he does state, "I have expressed my opinion and I won't step back." (TV 12)

5/20 Commenting on the Jesuit case, the Bishop Rosa Chávez says, "we hope that this grotesque act will finally put an end to impunity which has been the norm until now. Although the Armed Forces deny persecution of the Church events prove otherwise. Some officers have sincere desires, but others continue with the same attitudes." (TV 12) "There are sectors that want to return to the past," he concludes. (YSU)

5/21 Air Force General Villamariona, a member of the Honor Commission, submits his written declaration to Judge Zamora. He says he was called by General Larios on January 5 and asked to participate in the Commission. According to his statement, which coincides with that of Colonel Machuca, the commission analyzed documentation, received reports from Colonel Rivas of the Special Investigation Unit, and recommended detention of the nine accused. He also says two members of the commission visited the UCA. (Sonora)

5/21 Judge Zamora will formally request the Commission report from President Cristiani, who admitted last week he had the document in his possession. (DH)

5/21 Colonel Ochóa Pérez submitted his statement on May 19, reaffirming his belief that Benavides acted "under orders." He explained the operational process: "To execute an order, first the information is received, then the situation is evaluated with a support or advisory group; a plan of action is elaborated and presented to superior officers then a decision is made and becomes operational orders. It is carried out by a military unit with sufficient capacity. This could not have been an exclusive action of Colonel Benavides."

"In my opinion, the deaths originated with the attitude of the extremist sectors due to the number of persons involved and the form of execution. It was a preconceived operation. The woman and her daughter were killed circumstantially." Ochóa says it is not true that he knows who was in the meeting that occurred just before the assassinations. "My statements on "Sixty Minutes," he concludes, "were possible due to the climate of freedom of expression encouraged by the efforts and the valiant example of President Alfredo Cristiani." (Declaration/DH)

5/21 Colonel Ciro López Roque rejects the Young Officers communique and the charges that Captain Chávez Garcia was executed by a Special Forces team. "He was killed in combat and now they are abusing his name. No one in the Armed Forces believes he was killed under orders. No one. The Armed Forces is very solid. The style of the document makes us think it could have been written by officers who deserted and joined the FMLN." (TV 6)

5/21 Jesuit José María Tojeira declares, "There is a conspiracy at the highest levels" to avoid resolution of the case. "A lot has not been investigated. The testimonies of the cadets were absurd. Many officers have been removed in transfers that cannot be considered "routine." (TV 6)

5/21 Supreme Court assigns Judge Oscar Arnoldo Romero to assist Judge Zamora; the Fourth Court received 1146 cases last year and 248 cases to date this year, all apart from the Jesuit case. (TV 6)

5/23 The missing log book from the Military School "has been found" and will be turned over to the judge, according to Cristiani. The report of the Honor Commission, which supposedly did not exist, will also be presented to the judge this week. Two of the officers from the Commission who ignored previous subpoenas expected to testify "soon." (LPG)

5/23 The Arms Control and Foreign Policy Caucus Report is "not important" says General Villamariona. "These Congress members come here for a few hours then write reports as though they are specialists or they come with the reports already written." Asked about the Jesuit investigation, he replies, "Only General Larios can talk about that." (TV 6)

5/24 The new International Director of AID, Dr. Ronald Roskins, visits El Salvador, meets with Cristiani and holds a press conference to express AID's "agreement with the nature and direction of government policies" and to inform the President of AID's intention to provide $98 million in balance-of-payments assistance, "depending on Congress." Roskins says he is aware of concern in the U.S. about human rights violations but "in our very frank discussion this morning with President Cristiani we were assured of his commitment to broaden the investigation (of the Jesuit case) and prosecution in the most professional and expeditious manner possible. He spoke with great conviction and I am personally convinced that the efforts will be carried out. While the objectives are uppermost and of grave importance to the country, obviously it is not the only item on the agenda in the context of a continuing war." (Sonora, TV 6, 12)

5/24 Supreme Court issues report on progress in the Jesuit case including: Colonel Carlos Avilés has been subpoenaed and U.S. Major Eric Buckland asked to submit a sworn testimony; President Cristiani requested to turn over the report off the Honor Commission; Héctor Úlises Cuenca Ocampo, the intelligence officer assigned to the DNI who participated in the November 13 search of the Jesuit house subpoenaed; second subpoenas issued for three military members of the Honor Commission, Lt. Col. Juan Equizabal, Major José Roberto Zamora and Capt. Juan Manuel Grijalva; the SIU has been asked to explain how the names of the four cadets were determined and Colonel Ricardo Sandoval of the Military School will be requested to explain who was responsible for the missing book and other controls that exist over personnel. (TV 12, YSU)

5/25 In Spain, the slain Jesuits and the UCA are honored with the prestigious Asturias Award, the Spanish equivalent of the Nobel Prize, for great efforts in human rights, dialogue and culture. (TV 6)

5/25 Attorney General Colorado says international pressures on the Jesuit case are "unacceptable." It is a very delicate case," he says, "We have been cautious. We want the truth to come out but we are not going to rely on Congress or any religious power. We must rely on our own conscience. Our duty is not to Congress but to the people." (TV 12)

5/28 The missing log book from the Military School has been burned, according to a report Judge Zamora has received from SIU Director, Colonel Rivas. Major Carlos Camilo Hérnandez, since promoted to Lieutenant Colonel, former Assistant Director of the Military School, allegedly gave the book to Lt. Yusshy Mendoza, one of the defendants in the case, sometime between December 1-16, in the middle of the night with instructions to destroy it. Mendoza and four unnamed cadets then allegedly burned the book. (TV 6, 12)

5/28 "The Judge must evaluate the situation," says President Cristiani, "If more are involved and there is merit they will be charged." Cristiani also informs the press that the Honor Commission report, dated January 12, was sent to the Judge yesterday. (TV 12)

5/28 The four cadets previously subpoenaed were not on duty November 15-16 after all, according to the judge's report, but December 15-16. "It was an involuntary error." The cadets actually on duty on the night of the assassinations were Elio Ernesto Munguia Guillen, Walter Danilo Merino, Gilberto Vanegas Zpeda and Norman Gilmar Larrama. The four will be subpoenaed: Munguia is currently serving with the First Brigade, Merino and Larrama are still with the Military School and Zepeda is with Military Detachment #6. (TV 6, 12, LPG 5/29)

5/29 "The evidence against the true authors [of the Jesuit assassinations] and all those who could be behind this crime is disappearing daily which, according to observers of the Catholic Church could carry serious international implications for El Salvador, given the mockery of justice in this case." (EM)

5/29 "The destruction of evidence is a crime in my country," says Ambassador Walker. "If this happened these people have to pay the bill." (TV 6, 12)

5/29 The President of the Supreme Court, Dr. Mauricio Gutierrez Castro "regrets the international pressure" in the Jesuit case. "A lot of wood has been thrown on the fire. They aren't allowing us to carry out a serious, calm investigation. Just ask the Jesuits if we are conducting a serious investigation. Logically, we have limitations. We are doing things that have never been done before in this country." (TV 12)

5/29 The Jesuit case is "one of the great national problems," says outgoing Attorney General Colorado. "If you ask me if I am totally convinced that the accused are guilty I would have to say no." Colorado agrees that "possibly" the crime was committed by military personnel." He also says there is "no way" to prosecute the Archbishop Romero case. "Too much time has passed. It will remain a mystery. How can you have scientific evidence after ten years?" (TV 12)

5/30 Two officers, members of the Honor Commission, appear in court after ignoring two subpoenas. Lt. Col. Juan Eguizabal and Major José Roberto Zamora arrive under heavy military security and testify for three hours behind closed doors, adding "nothing new" to the case according to defense attorney Carlos Méndez who adds that there is no evidence against his clients and "a lot is lacking in order to bring the case to trial." (TV 6) Six of the seven members of the commission have testified or presented sworn declarations. The lack of information provided "could neutralize the efforts of the judge," according to the reporter. (TV 12)

5/30 Attorney General Mauricio Colorado will end his term tomorrow. ARENA will reportedly propose Dr. Roberto Mendoza, who served as Vice-Foreign Minister during the Romero Government, as new Attorney General. (TV 12)

5/31 Human Rights Commission publishes a letter to Cristiani, including a copy of a letter written by César Joya Mártinez to Ambassador Walker on May 18, in which Mártinez expresses his willingness to collaborate in the investigation of the Jesuit case:

"I have chosen an open letter in an attempt to avoid further delays in making my testimony public."

"I believe that because of this delay six Jesuit priests and two women are dead. Moreover I believe that if I had not escaped from the intelligence unit of the First Brigade in San Salvador, I would have been one of those sent by my superiors to kill them."

"As you well know, Mr. Ambassador, I have offered repeatedly and in written form to submit to the most rigorous interrogations (with legal guarantees and on the record), publicly and formally, about my activities as an intelligence officer in cases attributed to the First Infantry Brigade."

"I offered this in a public press conference on November 1, 1989, as well as in a letter personally delivered to you by Congressmember Joe Moakley of the Special Task Force on El Salvador, February 9, 1990."

"I myself was involved in the vigilance of the assassinated priests. The intelligence structures to which I belonged were directly involved in said assassinations. There were two U.S. advisors assigned to my unit. I believe that the Jesuits would possibly be alive if the government of the United States had acted to investigate the very clear statements that I made for the first time October 26, 1989 on the CBS Evening News."

"As you said in the *Washington Post* October 27, 1989, "The charges are very sensational and serious. We have been urging the government and armed forces to clarify this in depth." It is my fervent desire that there be an exhaustive and immediate investigation and clarification of these events. I wish that we could advance in this common task. I fear that the longer it is delayed, more assassinations will resuLt. After months of preparation and negotiations I would think that your office would be capable of scheduling an inquiry within the next two weeks. I urge that it be arranged." Copies of the letter were sent to James Baker, Richard Cheney, General Colin Powell and William Webster. (LPG 5/31/90)

5/31 Colonel Elena Fuentes says the charges made by César Joya Mártinez have "no basis" and are a "tactic of the FMLN to discredit the government and the Armed Forces. They are activating the international disinformation front, as evidenced by his efforts to discredit the military. If they have proof they should present it." (DH)

5/31 In West Germany, Miguel Estrada, Rector of the UCA, calls on the U.S. Government to pressure the Salvadoran military to collaborate in the investigation of the Jesuit assassinations. "I believe that only the U.S. can accomplish this." The West German Government is "studying the possibility of exerting pressure" on the Cristiani government to respect human rights and complete the investigation; pressure could include an end to all aid to the government. (DL)

5/31 The burning of the log book, says Rubén Zamora "indicates a clear intent to implement a cover-up. As long as this continues, democracy cannot exist in the country." (YSU)

June 1990

6/1 The Honor Commission did not receive any testimonies, confessions or evidence that Colonel Benavides participated in the Jesuit assassinations, according to the declarations of Lt. Col. Juan Vicente Eguizabal who says the Commission only analyzed documents and "called on everyone to tell the truth." General Villamariona and Colonel Machuca were responsible to exhort Benavides to tell the truth "but he remained silent." Eguizabal says the Commission first met on January 6 in National Police Headquarters and received reports on ballistics tests from SIU Director Colonel Rivas. Two members of the Commission visited the UCA then the Commission met with thirty members of the military; no questions were asked. (DH)

6/1 Heavy security around the court buildings as two military officers appear to present declarations. Neither Lt. Héctor Ulises Cuenca Ocampo, member of the DIN (National Intelligence Agency) or Captain Juan Manuel Grijalva of the Honor Commission present new evidence, according to a court official. Cuenca, who participated in the search of the Jesuit house on November 13, admits his participation "under orders" from his superior officer, Captain Herrera Carranza. (YSU, TV 12) Colonel Carlos Avilés scheduled to appear in court on June 4th. (EM) Journalists prevented from entering the area protest to court officials who inform them the restrictions were not ordered by the Lower Court or the Supreme Court but the Armed Forces. "It is a priority for us to give attention to the press," says a representative of the Attorney General's office. "They should understand," states the reporter, "that these impediments only affect the national and international credibility of the process." (TV 12)

6/3 Archbishop Rivera y Damas severely criticizes the ARENA government, saying . . . Justice has once again been mocked with the disappearance of evidence in the Jesuit case.

6/4 An administrative employee of the Military School who was in charge of the missing log book testifies today that the book was taken by Lt. Yusshy Mendozza and four cadets under orders of Captain Camilo Hérnandez; he says he was informed that the book would be burned. (TV 12)

6/4 Reporter covering the Jesuit case in the courthouse today notes that restrictions against the press were lessened and that there is a new attitude from the Attorney General's office toward the press, "probably due to the new Attorney General." (TV 12)

6/4 The archivist from the Military School who testified this morning, Juan René Arana Aguilar, declared that he was ordered by Captain (now Lt. Col.) Camilo Hérnandez to give all the registration books, "more than 70," from 1989 to Lt. Yusshy Mendoza who, accompanied by four cadets, destroyed them. According to the testimony "it was not routine to destroy the books." This was the first occasion during the years he has held the position that records have been destroyed. Representative of the Attorney General's office, Sidney Blanco, tells the press the testimony is "very important." "The books were destroyed during the period December 1-16, which means that personnel of the Military School were already suspects in the case early in December." Lt. Col. Camilo Hérnandez, now serving as Executive Officer in the Belloso Battalion, will be subpoenaed and could be charged with destruction of evidence, as could Lt. Mendoza. (DH 6/5)

6/4 Captain David Koch Arana, paymaster from the Minister of Defense assigned to the Military School, also testifies today and the court reports receiving the sworn testimony of U.S. advisor Major Eric Buckland. (DH)

6/4 Colonel Carlos Avilés scheduled to testify today but is reportedly in Taiwan for a two-month training course. (YSU)

6/6 Lt. Yusshy Mendoza appears in court today under extremely heavy military security, "more than Cristiani," according to one court employee. He testifies for three hours about the missing registration books. According to his defense attorney, "It's all routine . . . They were a series of unimportant books . . . The destruction was just routine." The press is pushed and shoved and some reporters hit by soldiers in the confusion. (TV 12) Mendoza says the burning of the books is "routine . . . for security reasons." (LPG 6/7) Henry Campos, one of the prosecuting attorneys, apologizes to the press for not providing information on the testimony, "for technical reasons I can't say more." (TV 6)

6/6 Col. (Ret.) Sigifredo Ochóa Pérez expresses concern about the destruction of the books and says the judge "should have all of our support." (DL) The case is advancing, says Ochóa, "only due to international pressure . . . but we also have our own laws." (TV 12)

6/6 Lt. Col. Oscar León Linares turns over command of the Atlacatl Battalion to Lt. Col. José Eduardo Angel Orellana. Linares, who commanded the Battalion during the offensive and on the night of the Jesuit assassinations, receives an award for having commanded the "loyal, seasoned and very Salvadoran" troops. He calls for a continuation of the struggle against the "common enemy . . . communism," and says, "We only used 50% of our troops to eradicate the terrorists from the northern perimeter of San Salvador." In November, Linares will take over Military Detachment #4 in Morazan. (DH)

6/6 The new Attorney General, Dr. Roberto Antonio Mendoza, takes over today; says he doesn't belong to any political party, that he will "guard respect for the law, for human rights and justice." (DL) He will be "zealous in compliance with the law in the entire country." (TV 6)

6/7 Judge Zamora releases press statement on the testimony of Lt. Yusshy Menndoza yesterday. The Lieutenant confessed to burning 70 books, under orders from Captain Camilio Hérnandez, who called him into his office on a date he does not recall in December. Accompanied by 3 or 4 cadets, "whose names he does not remember," he took the books to the incinerator at about 10:00 pm and burned them. He claims that since computers were introduced in 1987, the registration books "are always burned." One book which registers all orders, arrests, promotions, etc., for the year "was taken to the National Police and turned over to some civilians." He does not know if that book was put on microfilm. (EM 6/7)

6/7 Minister of Defense Larios affirms that it is "normal" to burn the books but this case is "suspicious" and must be investigated. General Villamariona agrees that it is "serious." (TV 12)

6/8 The sworn statement of U.S. Major Eric Buckland, dated January 3, was received by the court earlier this week. According to Buckland, he was in the office of Colonel Carlos Avilés on December 20, "talking about the psychological operations . . . a normal chat that we had almost daily." "This time he (Avilés) said he had additional information about the Jesuit assassinations and confided that he must let it be known in case of emergency." Buckland says that Avilés informed him that Colonel Ivan López y López had confided to him that Lt. Col. Manuel Antonio Rivas (Director of the SIU) said that Benavides had accepted responsibility for the crime. "Later, when the investigation began, Colonel Benavides said to Rivas, 'I did it . . . What can you do to help me?'" Avilés said Rivas was frightened and didn't know what to do . . . As a result the investigation slowed down because López y López was Rivas' advisor." Colonel Avilés allegedly told Buckland that no one else knew but "it was likely that Ponce had the information but Avilés wasn't certain." Buckland says he wanted to know why Benavides wasn't arrested and Avilés told him it couldn't be done until the investigation was concluded. Avilés also told him he had seen Benavides in the Military School and "he looked as though he wasn't eating, had lost weight and was upset." (LPG) According to Diario de Hoy, Buckland also says in his testimony that Avilés confided to him that members of the Atlacatl Battalion, commanded by a lieutenant, had committed the crime and later said the investigation was "going well," that a lieutenant of the Atlacatl "did poorly" on the lie detector test, and "seemed nervous and made excuses about the tests." (DH)

6/8 FMLN releases a statement charging the government and military with opposing negotiations or looking for "an easy negotiation," and with a lack of willingness to investigate and prosecute crimes such as Archbishop Romero, the Jesuits and San Sebastian. (TV 12)

6/8 Two of the four cadets allegedly on duty in the Military School November 15-16 appear in court today and present declarations; Walter

Danilo Merino, still assigned to the Military School, and Elio Ernesto Munguia Guillen, now assigned to the First Brigade, arrive under heavy military security and "offer nothing new" according to first reports. (TV 12)

6/8 The two cadets who testified this morning were on duty November 15-16 but "don't remember anything" and provided "no important information." TV reporter says "there seems to be a collective amnesia," and notes the "athletic capacity" of the cadets as they flee the press to jump in military vehicles after their declarations. (TV 6)

6/11 Lt. Elio Ernesto Munguia, 24, one of the cadets from the Military School who testified on June 8, said he was on duty from 7:00 am November 15 to 7:00 am November 16 but that not all comings and goings had been entered into the log book "due to the abnormal situation"; he had made notes on a piece of paper which he had given to the Guard Commander who maintained a separate book. He declared that about 200 soldiers were on the grounds of the School that night from the Atlacatl, Cavalry, Artillery, Marines, Military Detachment 6 & 7 units. The second cadet, Lt. Walter Albert Merino relieved Munguia during his rest periods and testified that he "didn't note anything . . . There was nothing unusual." (DH 6/12) Merino stayed in a room near the gate when he was not relieving Munguia; he testified that he never saw Lt. Mendoza. (EM) Munguia said that Colonel Benavides kept the log book of entries and exits of troops on combat missions, as well as his personal log book. He was relieved three times during the night, and slept from 1:00 - 5:00 am, but "didn't remember who relieved him." He didn't know anything about an incinerator on the premises. Judge Zamora has requested the Minister of Defense to provide a copy of the alleged 1987 instructions to burn all log books. (TV 12, LPG 6/12) The Judge has also subpoenaed Lt. Col. Camilo Hérnandez, the officer who ordered the destruction of the books. Two more cadets on duty that night will testify June 18th. (DL)

6/12 The new Attorney General, Roberto Mendoza, visits the President of the National Assembly then announces a "new strategy" in the Jesuit case but does not specify what the strategy is. He tells *Diario de Hoy* that he has not been "pressured" by anyone but the paper comments

on the "great international pressure" in the Jesuit case . . . "Many sectors
are taking advantage of the case to propagandize against El Salvador . . .
making all the people responsible for a crime committed by a few delinquents . . . No one remembers such a persistent and poisonous campaign
as this one." (DH 6/13)

6/12 A fourth "Young Officers Letter" is distributed in the capital:

"We demand that the assassination of Héctor Oqueli Colíndres be
uncovered as well as the Jesuit assassinations . . . And that Colonel Denis
Moran be brought to the country immediately."

"We oppose the formation of Honor Commissions in the Armed
Forces whose participants respond to orders from the High Command . . .
which is why these crimes are never clarified . . . The arrest of Benavides
and the other officers was part of an arranged conspiracy . . . Everyone
knows at a professional level that the testimonies of co-defendants are
inadmissible . . . otherwise the Honor commission would not have recommended the arrest of Benavides and the officers who only obeyed orders."

"We are waiting to see Colonel Denis Moran returned to the country,
and we appeal to Brigade Executive Officers, Department heads, Intelligence and Operations units of all Brigades to pressure for justice in both
cases if we want to conserve the Institution."

"Don't be surprised if the members of the 35th Promotion (the Tandona) say that the Young Officers Command doesn't exist . . . For obvious reasons we can't be known . . . We will exist clandestinely until it
is time to go public . . . We are growing and collecting evidence to punish the corrupt . . . so the people will have confidence in their institution."
(DL)

6/13 Radio Venceremos on the Jesuit case: The destruction of evidence, etc., "demonstrate that it was the High Command that ordered the
crime and Benavides who carried it out . . . The trial is at a standstill and
there are no indications that the case will be prosecuted; to the contrary,
the possibility exists that the only high-ranking officer will be released."

6/13 Two cadets testify in court today on the Jesuit case. Norman
Gilmar Larama and Gilberto Vanegas Zépeda "have no further information," because they were on duty from 7:00 am November 16th to 7:00

am November 17th. The Defense Attorney still insists the case must be moved to Santa Tecla. (TV 6) Lt. Colonel Camilo Hérnandez will appear in court on June 15th; representative of Attorney General's office says his testimony will be "very important." (EM)

6/15 Lt. Colonel Carlos Camilo Hérnandez appears in court at 8:00 am to testify in the Jesuit case. Lt. Yusshy Mendoza has testified that Hérnandez, now Executive Officer of the Belloso Battalion, gave the order to destroy the log books in the Military School. No information yet available on his testimony. (TV 12)

6/15 Lt. Col. Camilo Hérnandez testifies for five hours but no information is released to the press on the contents of his statement. (TV 6)

6/15 COACES calls for a reduction of the armed forces "so the cost is no greater than 10% of the national budget, an end to forced recruitment, an end to impunity and prosecution for those responsible for the El Mozóte, Sumpúl, Las Hojas, San Sebastián, FENASTRAS and UCA massacres, purification of the military, elimination of all 'untouchable and immune autonomous structures' of the military and elimination of all paramilitary and clandestine structures." (DL)

6/17 Archbishop Rivera y Damas says, "the people know who is responsible for the Jesuit assassinations."

6/18 In his declaration to the court on June 15th Lt. Colonel Camilo Hérnandez, Assistant Director of the Military School in November, denied ordering the destruction of the log books. He admitted that he had asked the archivist about the books. (TV 12) He asked about the books during the first week of December he said, because Colonel Benavides had asked him and he "does not remember" ordering that the book of orders be taken to the National Police. He said that "days" before the crime Benavides attended a meeting at the High Command and then met with all officers, including Lt. Yusshy Mendoza, but only discussed the offensive. The Security Command under control of Benavides included troops from Military Detachments 6 and 7, Cavalry, Artillery and Military Police. The court has also received a statement from Minister of

Defense Larios and Colonel Ricardo Casanova Sandoval, current head of the Military School, that contrary to earlier testimony, no order has existed since 1987 to destroy all log books. (DH 6/19)

6/18 According to the testimony of Hérnandez the Security Command was broken down into four units: S1 - personnel; S2 - Information; S3 - operations; and S4 - logistics. He said, "I don't know why Arana and Méndez involved me in this . . . I believe they both are lying." Lt. Col. Manuel Rivas, Director of the SIU, requested the Order Book and it was apparently delivered to him at the National Police. (DL 6/19)

6/20 Sixteen officers of the DNI [National Intelligence Agency] have testified to the SIU about the meeting on the morning of November 16; Colonel Ponce gave a list of names of the officers to the Investigation Unit. All sixteen denied that "cheering" occurred when Captain Carlos Carranza informed them of the Jesuit assassinations. (YSU) Those interviewed included Captain David Koch Arana and Lt. Héctor Ulises Cuenca Ocampo. Colonel Mauricio Guzmán Aguilar and Captain Luís Alberto Parada Fuentes, participants in the meeting, are out of the country and were not interviewed. Guzmán Aguilar is in Costa Rica as Military Attaché and Parada Fuentes is attending the School of the Americas in the US. (LPG)

6/20 Press waits in the courthouse all day for Colonel Carlos Avilés to testify in the Jesuit case but he does not appear and apparently is still in Taiwan. His testimony is considered "very important." (DL) A prosecuting attorney says the only evidence against Benavides is that the troops who committed the massacre were under his command and the weapons belonged to the Military School. "He had to authorize the troops and the weapons." (DH 6/21)

6/20 On June 14, the European Parliament passed a resolution denouncing obstacles in the investigation and demanding prosecution of the Jesuit and Héctor Oquelí cases. (EM)

6/21 Prosecuting attorneys in the Jesuit case have been receiving death threats "in recent days," according to sources close to the case but the attorneys cautiously deny the report. "Anything can happen in this country," says Eduardo Pineda Valenzuela. "We are used to having problems . . . and this is the most important case in the history of the country." Reporter says the threats are serious and "some humanitarian organizations" have the information. (TV 12)

6/21 "We are all in danger," says another attorney. "but we have made a commitment to justice because we are patriotic and this is a case that affects the people." Asked about Judge Ricardo Zamora, he responds, "I think that a fearful or comfortable judge would have resigned . . . The fact that he is still here is a credit to his determination." Zamora, 45, is said to be a calm, deeply religious man. The prosecuting attorney also says that Lt. Col. Camilo Hérnandez could be arrested for destruction of evidence "if it is proven." He declines to predict any timetable for continuation of the case. (DL)

6/21 Father Francisco Ibizate of the UCA says the case is being blocked and progress is not satisfactory. "It is a vicious circle," he says. "By discovering little we are discovering a lot . . . Internationally, the image is very bad." (TV 12)

6/22 Vargas admits that the military has enjoyed impunity but "it is not the dominion of the military, rather a peculiarity of the judicial system." (DL 6/23)

6/23 U.S. State Department report on terrorism accuses the FMLN of responsibility for nine incidents of terrorism during 1989, denounces the "inadequate judicial system," the "terror of the ultra-right and/or the Armed Forces," and says, "some incidents could be attributed to the Armed Forces," including the Jesuit case. (EM)

6/26 Jesuit Provincial Tojeira denounces efforts to block the investigation of the Jesuit case, "to try only the nine and eliminate the participation of the intellectual authors . . . If they are not blocking it why did they burn the books? . . . There were 219 soldiers around the UCA that night who didn't see or hear anything . . . Two soldiers were in the Democratic Tower . . . who did not see the Bengal lights . . . There are a series of contradictions which lead us to believe that the case will end with the nine 'black sheep' . . . but the killings put the issue of impunity in crisis in this country." (TV 12)

6/27 Judge Ricardo Zamora orders detention of Lt. Colonel Camilo Hérnandez, former Assistant Director of the Military School, for destruction of evidence. Colonel Carlos Avilés appears to testify but does not meet with the press, saying, "Only the Minister of Defense and the President can make statements . . . I will declare what I know." (TV 12) The book of orders, reportedly containing 500 files beginning September 13, was turned over to the court yesterday. (TV 12, DL)

6/27 President of the Supreme Court Dr. Mauricio Gutierrez says Judge Zamora is "working seriously," carrying out a "serious, responsible investigation, slow but sure." (TV 6)

6/28 U.S. House of Representatives approves a bill withholding 50% of military aid; Republicans do not attempt to block the legislation, which now goes to the Senate and could still be vetoed by President Bush. Under the terms of the legislation the 50% could be reinstated if the FMLN launches an offensive or does not negotiate "in good faith." All aid will be eliminated if the government does not negotiate seriously or if the Jesuit case is not resolved. (DL)

6/29 Portions of Colonel Carlos Avilés' declaration are published in *Diario Latino*; Avilés denied he told U.S. Major Buckland anything he heard from Colonel López y López about Benavides. He said he knew Buckland for a year, that the two met in December "as usual, for reasons of work," that he [Avilés] took a lie detector test with North Americans present which had questionable results due to his "state of mind." On January 2, according to his testimony, Colonel Ponce called him in with Buckland and US Colonel Menjivar; he asked Buckland to clarify what he had said and Buckland asked to talk to Menjivar alone but the Colonel refused. Buckland then said he "didn't know why" he had made the comment [that Avilés told him] about the confession of Benavides to Rivas. Avilés "rebuked" him and told him that the accusation could cost him his career, the security of his family and himself. "Buckland was silent, then ambiguous," said Avilés, "I haven't seen him since . . . I wish I had a crystal ball to know why this major made the assertion . . . I prefer to think he was out of his mind due to the war . . . I have no knowledge that Benavides confessed to Rivas or anyone else." Avilés said he saw Benavides after November 16th in the High Command but did not discuss the case, that he was in the November 15th meeting from 8:00-9:00 pm in the High Command but doesn't remember if Benavides was present; during the meeting the offensive was analyzed, "but no orders were given" and there was "no discussion about the FMLN inside the UCA." The 7:00 am meeting on the 16th was "routine" and Avilés says he "did not know about the crime until he heard the news on a commercial radio station." (DL 6/29)

6/29 Avilés' statement "complicates the case," says a prosecuting attorney. "The possibilities now that the accused will ever go to trial are 10% . . . and zero percent that they will be convicted." (EM 6/29)

July 1990

7/2   Colonel Benavides appears in court at 8:30 am under heavy guard, "too ill to testify," reportedly suffering from laryngitis and a stomach infection. He was subpoenaed to respond to questions about the destruction of the log books and will be called again. Defense attorneys tell reporters Benavides has a note from his doctor affirming his illness. (TV 6)

7/2   Defense attorney's appeal for Lt. Colonel Camilo Hérnandez is denied by Judge Zamora who orders his detention. (TV 12)

7/4   Two officers testify today in the Jesuit case, Captain Julio Armando Garcia Oliva and Major Herberto Oswaldo Vides Lucha; both served in the Special Commands operating out of the Military School during the offensive and "provide no new information." (TV 6)

7/4   Ambassador Walker is "concerned" about the Jesuit case, "because I have the impression it is going slow; but I have confidence in the President and that the country wants the truth." Walker says he is "more confident" about the negotiations, "I have the impression that many things will be discussed . . . There are problems . . . I have a lot of confidence in the President, the people and sectors that want the war to end." He says he is "cautious" about U.S. aid, "I can't predict how Congress will act." (TV 12)

7/5   Court officials say the defense in the Jesuit case is using "a strategy of providing false information to the press" and warning journalists to be cautious when reporting. Citing the case of the alleged illness of Colonel Benavides, officials say "it is not true that he presented a medical certification of illness . . . He simply said his throat hurt and he had intestinal problems." Benavides will appear again next Wednesday; Colonel Manuel Antonio Rivas and Colonel Ivan López y López will both be subpoenaed. (EM)

7/5 The Attorney General denies that anyone involved in prosecuting the Jesuit case has been threatened. In response to a report from an international press service that Benavides is at the beach, the official says, "I don't know where he is . . . I couldn't say whether he is in Mariona or where." (TV 6)

7/5 According to the Minister of Defense, the arrest warrant for Lt. Col. Camilo Hérnandez was just received today and the detention has been ordered. (TV 6)

7/6 Colonel René Emilio Ponce, speaking at the American Chamber of Commerce breakfast on "The Role of the Armed Forces in the Dialogue-Negotiation Process," says Lt. Colonel Camilo Hérnandez was placed under arrest yesterday "as soon as detention orders were received" and is being held in the National Guard, charged with "concealing evidence," with a 25,000 colón embargo on his personal property. (TV 12)

7/6 According to the testimony of Major Herbert Oswaldo Vides Lucha (July 4), he was head of Section II of the Security Command of the zone which included the Ministry of Defense, the High Command, and the Military School during the offensive, and is now stationed in the Studies Center of the Armed Forces. During the offensive, he was in the Center of Technical Operations of the Military School under the responsibility of Lt. Col. Camilo Hérnandez; his section was responsible for the book of daily operations until it was disbanded in January, and responsibility for the book was turned over to Captain Fuentes Rodas. He said he did not know if anyone from the Military School participated in the raid of the Jesuit house on November 13; he was only responsible for communicating with cadets entering or leaving the School, "but all orders came from Colonel Benavides." He "doesn't know" if members of the Atlacatl Battalion were in the school. He said he heard about the Jesuit assassinations from the newspaper. "When a member of the military is under the orders of a commander and commits a crime," he said, "the commander must also respond because all orders come from him." (DL, EM)

7/6 Judge Zamora apparently has the "order book" and photocopies of the operations books, according to a defense attorney. (TV 6)

7/6 Two more officers testify today, a Captain Miguel Castillo and Captain Fuentes Rodas, providing "no new details," according to a prosecuting attorney. (TV 6)

7/10 Urban Commandos "Modesto Ramírez" calls local radio stations and take responsibility for the assassination of Major Figueroa yesterday. (Sonora)

7/10 Bernard Aronson arrives on the afternoon flight; meets with President Cristiani and the dialogue commission, accompanied by Ambassador Walker and other Embassy officials; he will reportedly express US concern about the Jesuit case, human rights and the negotiations. (TV 12)

7/11 Colonel Benavides testifies for six hours today, "providing new information," according to a prosecuting attorney, "more evidence of his innocence," says defense attorney Carlos Castellón. The notorious "order book" is shown to Benavides and he affirms its authenticity. (TV 12) As he is leaving under heavy guard the Colonel says to reporters, "The investigation continues on course and justice will prevail at the end." (DH 7/12)

7/11 An official of the Attorney General's office says the Colonel is "sharing a cell" with 3 or 4 other persons and is allowed outside for one hour a day. "He should be moved to Mariona as requested by the Attorney General." (EM)

7/11 Lt. Colonel Camilo Hérnandez, now also under arrest in the Jesuit case, also testifies in court today. (DL)

7/11 Bernard Aronson says . . . the Armed Forces must not tolerate officers or soldiers who violate the law, abuse human rights or are corrupt . . . independent of the position of the FMLN in the dialogue. (LPG 7/12)

7/11 On the Jesuit investigation Aronson says it is advancing but there is "no doubt that the United States will not be satisfied unless there is a complete investigation and an impartial trial." (TV 12)

7/12 President Cristiani holds a press conference to discuss a number of issues:

Jesuit case: A reporter asks if the High Command should not also be fired, to facilitate investigation of the Jesuit assassinations. "There are no parallels," he responds, "they are collaborating in the investigation." He is then asked to comment on Colonel Benavides' statement to the court that the order to search the UCA came from the High Command, and Cristiani admits, for the first time, that the order did come from the High Command and was authorized by him, "Armed subversives had been seen entering . . . Arms and uniforms were found inside . . . but this did not mean that the entire Jesuit University was terrorist." He also says the Atlacatl Battalion was not yet under orders of Colonel Benavides on the 13th, the day of the search, but was still directly under the High Command. (LPG 7/13)

7/12 Yesterday, Colonel Benavides denied all charges against him, saying he heard loud explosions near the UCA early in the morning of the 16th of November, but he "wasn't certain exactly where and no one reported the situation on the radio." He found out about the assassinations later in the morning and in the afternoon met with other officers. He stated that he did not order an investigation, because his orders were to defend the military installations in the zone and not to carry out missions. He did not order the search of the UCA or surveillance in the area during the offensive. He "doesn't remember" any book burning, but said there is an incinerator on the premises; all books were microfilmed, (DL) "but he never saw the microfilm." (EM) "He did not order any missions on the night of the 15th-16th and was aware only of one confrontation in Antiguo Cuscatlán. He affirmed that all units under his command were in direct radio contact with the High Command and that Major Camilo Hérnandez as chief of staff of the special command unit of the Military School could give orders on his own initiative or rather retransmit those of the Colonel." He says his commanding officers met every 24 hours and Major Miguel Castillo explained the operations log at those meetings. (LPG 7/13)

7/12 A prosecuting attorney says Benavides' testimony is "full of contradictions." For example, "No military unit could leave the School without his knowledge but he admitted the units did not always report to him." The Atlacatl unit "should have reported to him, but didn't." The search of the UCA "could only have been ordered by the Chief of Staff," (Colonel Ponce), says the attorney. (EM)

7/12 Bush Administration will offer a compromise bill to Congressional Democrats, reducing aid 15-30% as of April 1991, including a total aid cut-off if the Cristiani government refuses to negotiate in good faith. The Administration says the Democratic proposal "provides scarce incentives to the FMLN to look for a resolution to the conflict"; the Bush proposal will withhold 15% until April, which will be released only if there is "significant progress in the Jesuit case"; another 15% will be withheld if the FMLN "accepts a truce, negotiates in good faith and ends all acts of terrorism." Total U.S. aid to date is over $5 billion. (EM/AP)

7/13 Captain Fernando Herrera Carranza, an intelligence officer from DNI [National Intelligence Department] testifies today in the Jesuit case that he ordered Lt. Héctor Úlises Cuenca Ocampo, also of DNI, to observe the raid on the Jesuit house November 13, which was led by Lt. José Ricardo Espinoza Guerra. Herrera said he "knew the search was the responsibility of the High Command but didn't know, as he does now, that it had been ordered by the High Command and authorized by President Cristiani." Prosecuting Attorney Sidney Blanco says today there are "new doubts" as a result of Benavides' testimony that he ordered the book burnings . . . "He repeated his total innocence." (EM)

7/14 Jesuit Provincial José María Tojeira believes Cristiani and Ponce have been "deceived" by other military officers . . . "There are many contradictions in the testimonies of the military . . . Unfortunately, the impression one has is of the great number of military personnel who have lied in their statements . . . Now it appears as though the raid of the UCA was authorized by Cristiani and Ponce, but I believe they have been deceived by their own officers who have lied to the judge because the raid on the 13th occurred at 6:30 pm, while and Ponce testified that he authorized the raid at 8:50 pm . . . I don't believe a Chief of Staff of the High Command could be mistaken when he gives a sworn statement to the judge." Tojeira also discards the statement of Cristiani that weapons and uniforms were found in the UCA during the raid. "I want to say that this is also a lie and part of the general deception of some members of the military who also participated in the assassinations. They began to say this eight months after the raid . . . No one said anything to me about it in spite of the fact that I had personal conversations with Cristiani and Ponce . . . They never mentioned weapons or uniforms . . . On the Sunday morning of the offensive (the 12th), two bombs were found because on Saturday night FMLN members fled through the UCA . . . The military took the bombs that day." (DL) The raid was a "reconnaissance mission prior to the crime," says Tojeira. (TV 12)

7/14   Tojeira also shows a letter from Congressman Joe Moakley denying a report in local press several weeks ago that the Task Force "spoke favorably" of the investigation. (TV 12)

7/14 According to the testimony of Captain Fernando Herrera Carranza yesterday (former head of operations of DNI), during the offensive he "rescued" the daughter of Cristiani from the "Albert Einstein" private university, "and was attacked by gunfire from inside the UCA." He said he was responsible for coordinating military operations to avoid confrontations between military patrols in the zone during the offensive. Herrera was the officer who reported the assassinations at the meeting of intelligence officials on the morning of the 16th. (EM)

7/14 A prosecuting attorney says, "it is strange to us that several days since the arrest of Lt. Col. Camilo Hérnandez by the National Guard, he still has not been brought to the court to testify." (LPG) The judge may subpoena Colonel Ponce again to testify as to who ordered the raid on the UCA. (DL)

7/15 During his Sunday homily, Msgr. Ricardo Urióste says he agrees with Jesuit Provincial Tojeira that "there are those interested in hiding certain things . . . They don't want to get to the bottom of it in spite of the evidence." (TV 12)

7/17 Defense attorney for Lt. Col. Carlos Camilo Hérnandez, Assistant Director of the Military School during the offensive, resigns after receiving death threats. Dr. Carlos Castellón says he received "moral coercion" from an "undefined sector." He files a petition with Judge Zamora asking that his client be released on bail and that his resignation be accepted. (TV 12)

7/17 Judge Zamora has subpoenaed Colonel Ivan López y López and Lt. Colonel Manuel Rivas; the court will request the Embassy to transmit subpoenas for U.S. Major Eric Buckland and Colonel Milton Menjivar. (TV 12)

7/17 Cristiani reproaches Jesuit Provincial Tojeira for his statement that the President and Colonel Ponce have been "deceived," saying, "This speculation is not constructive. (The information) has never been hidden. The raid was to investigate if the FMLN was moving through the UCA." (TV 12)

7/17 Vice-President Merino says the investigation is "going well," in spite of comments by Tojeira. "You have to be careful with these priests who criticize." (TV 12)

7/18 Lt. Colonel Carlos Camilo Hérnandez appears in court this morning; tells reporters, "I have confidence in God, in justice and in my innocence . . . I didn't order any illegal actions." Hérnandez does not testify today because he does not have a defense attorney, but attorneys for Colonel Benavides will take his case; one of them, Carlos Méndez Flores, refuses to answer press questions, saying, "There is too much speculation going on." The reporter comments, "There are too many contradictions in this case . . . Even President Cristiani admitted only a few days ago that he had authorized the raid on the UCA." (TV 6)

7/18 Jesuit Provincial Tojeira suggests the military should make its own internal investigation of the case. "If I were in the military I would like the truth to come out. For its own good an internal investigation must be promoted." He also says, "The assassinations . . . must be seen in the context of 75, 000 deaths . . . If in some way these deaths [the Jesuits] have had international repercussions, it is because they have contributed to opening eyes about the enormous number of unjust deaths in El Salvador." (DL)

7/19 Conservative Bishop Romeo Tovar Astorga denounces the assassinations of two military officers during recent weeks and says, "These assassinations balance the Jesuit assassinations, they are equalized . . . Unfortunately, the balance of injustice is equalized. Now we must equalize justice." (TV 6, 12)

7/19 Judge Zamora will subpoena UCA Rector Francisco Estrada to testify as a victim in the case. He has also requested Minister of Defense Larios to provide a list of names of all members of the Atlacatl Battalion assigned to the Military School on November 13th. (DL) The list must include the names of the drivers who transported troops to the School. (TV 12) Colonel Ponce has been subpoenaed but will be required only to present a written statement. (TV 12)

7/20 A statement from the General Command of the FMLN comments on the Jesuit assassinations:

"With his confession of having ordered the raid of the Jesuit residence two days before the assassinations, President Cristiani has a political responsibility for the crime. The concrete act cannot be separated from the political framework which surrounded it. For example: Who ordered and politically oriented the National Network to attack and threaten the Jesuits and all opposition with death at the moment when the President ordered raids on their houses and offices?"

"From the most recent information it is evident that Cristiani himself participated in the decision or induced others, and that Colonel Ponce was the intellectual executive of the crime, with other high-ranking officers . . . In El Salvador no one is surprised that colonels or rightist presidents order massacres, but in the current national and international political context, it is a scandal and an unusual act that cannot be tolerated . . . and it has a direct relation to the real possibility of a negotiated solution to the war."

"We hope that in the San José meeting the government provides evidence that the Jesuit case will be resolved. Without a resolution of this case the negotiation is morally and politically blocked." (DL)

7/20 Roberto D'Aubuisson on the Jesuit case:

"I believe that some will be convicted for the act itself. It did not discredit the Armed Forces, it discredits those who committed the act." (Sonora) "It is strange that on this occasion they haven't accused me." (EM)

7/20 Francisco Estrada, Rector of the UCA, testifies in court today and later meets with the press. "It is difficult to believe they will get to the bottom of the case," he says, "the contradictions show that something serious is being hidden." The report that weapons were found in the UCA is "ridiculous." (EM) As a priest and as a Christian, I believe in pardon and I think my dead *compañeros* would be willing to pardon. But first there must be truth, then justice. Then we will talk about forgiveness." (TV 12) "I doubt that we will get to the intellectual authors . . . but the truth must prevail." (TV 6)

7/22 Archbishop Rivera y Damas, during his Sunday Homily, says that the Jesuit case, "is not just another case. It is the key case . . . The credibility of the government and Armed Forces depend on its resolution." (TV 12)

7/22 Guancorito, Chalatenango, renamed "Ciudad Ignacio Ellacuría" today during ceremony attended by religious and political leaders, the press and members of the FMLN. Father Jon Sobrino says, "For us, it is an honor that these people who have suffered so much have chosen to immortalize Father Ellacuría." Eighty families repopulated Guancorita last October; the community was bombed by the Air Force in February. One old woman interviewed by a journalist expresses her joy on the occasion; asked if she has lost any family members during the war, she replies, "My brothers, my son and my husband." (TV 12) FMLN Commander Salvador Guerra says there will be a cease-fire by the end of the year. (TV 12, Buenos Dias)

7/23 The FMLN proposal presented in Mexico includes:

1. Elimination of the death squads

2. Disbanding of all paramilitary structures

3. An end to forced recruitment

4. Expulsion of all officers accused of torture and assassination—approximately 200, 10% of the officer corps. Prosecution of four cases: Jesuits, Msgr. Romero, Héctor Oquelí and FENASTRAS, as examples to end impunity.

5. Dismantling of the National Guard, Treasury Police, Panther Battalion and Atlacatl Battalion.

6. Elimination of the DNI

7. Appointments of Vice-Ministers of Defense and Security by consensus, including the FMLN.

8. Restructuring of National Police to include elimination of all S-2 (intelligence) structures, to be converted to Human Rights offices. (EM 7/21)

7/23 For the third time, defense attorneys in the Jesuit case are attempting to move the case to the Santa Tecla court, citing Article 283 of the Criminal Code. The judge has three days to rule on the request and will solicit an opinion from the Attorney General's office. (TV 12)

7/24 Judge Zamora hopes for a response by July 30 to his request that U.S. Major Buckland and Colonel Menjivar testify. (DH) Lt. Col. Camilo Hérnandez will testify on the 27th. (DL)

7/25 "Cristiani's credibility has been affected by his admission that he ordered the raid on the Jesuit house," says Shafik Handal. "This means that the President hid important information for seven months . . . and raises other questions . . . No one can believe that he doesn't know more. We believe he knows everything, he is the Commander-in-Chief." (Horizonte)

7/25 *La Prensa Grafica* publishes a version of the 33-point government proposal, "The Role of the Armed Forces in the Democratic System," "leaked" to the press yesterday. According to this report the government is proposing:

1. Define the role of the Armed Forces in the democratic society

2. A plan of education and awareness on the interests of the Armed Forces

3. Promotion of "civic-military" seminars among official and private sectors

4. Full ratification of the principles of Esquipulas II

5. Support for the negotiations in matters of security, unification, control and arms limitations for Central America

6. Support for pending legal processes in the cases of Msgr. Romero, the Jesuits, FENASTRAS, Héctor Oquelí, assassinated mayors, Dr. Rodriguez Porth, Dr. Francisco Peccorini and Zona Rosa

7. "Negative" members of the Armed Forces to be submitted to a military tribunal

8. A law of control and regulation of private security groups

9. Legal collection of all weapons exclusively for use of the Armed Forces

10. Executive Decree to suspend permission for private persons to carry weapons of the Armed Forces

11. Eradication of all forms of "private justice"

12. Ley de Punto Final, with the exception of the cases in #6

13. Punishment to violators of the agreements reached in these proposals

14. Reforms to the law to punish illicit earnings, to include the commanders of military units

15. Mechanisms to supervise the Armed Forces

16. Law to regulate the provisions of the Armed Forces, according to the budget

17. Establish regulations for the Inspector General

18. Creation of an Honor Tribunal

19. Creation of a committee to review legislation of the Armed Forces

20. Creation of a committee of doctrine and education

21. Military University
22. Creation of human rights offices of the Armed Forces
23. Control of the intelligence structure by the president
24. Transfer elite battalions to the brigade commanders
25. Transfer National Police and National Guard
26. Transfer Treasury Police to Ministry of Treasury
27. Transfer Panther, Liberatadores, 15 de Septiembre and CEAT battalions to the army
28. Advisors (international?) to administer paramilitary forces or civil defense
29. Disarm civil defense
30. Disband civil defense
31. Law of military conscriptions
32. Redefinition of the objective of military service
33. Suspension of recruitment on signing of cease-fire.

NOTE: This was translated as printed in *La Prensa Grafica*.

7/26 In Costa Rica, Shafik Handal releases a letter from the FMLN General Command to President Cristiani accusing him of political responsibility for the Jesuit assassinations, based on his own admission that he authorized the raid on November 13, "In any democratic country, you and your High Command would be asked to resign." (TV 12, Horizonte)

Lic. Alfredo Cristiani:

"You acknowledged to the press that you authorized the raid of the UCA on November 13, 1989, and that this order was issued by the Chief of Staff of the High Command, Colonel René Emilio Ponce."

"Pressured by the development of the circumstances surrounding the case of the Jesuits, you have revealed an element that you kept hidden and that is essential in order to establish responsibility for this horrendous crime."

"In ordering this raid, you and the High Command took a decisive step in the chain of decisions and orders that led, three days later, to the assassination of the Jesuit priests."

"Independently of the final result of the criminal and legal process relative to this crime, your political responsibility, Mr. Cristiani, has been established by these statements."

"The responsibility of Colonel Ponce and all of the High Command was established from the beginning when it was accepted that the Armed Forces committed the crime."

"Your delayed public confession makes the following conclusions evident and unavoidable:

1. If you were capable of hiding the truth of your responsibility in the raid for seven months, there is sufficient basis to suppose that you know a great deal more, including everything related to the decisions, the intellectual authors and the executioners of the brutal massacre.

2. It is public knowledge that you met continuously with Colonel Ponce and other members of the High Command during our offensive of November 1989, and that the National Radio and Television Network, imposed by your government during those days, had your authorization; the official voice of this Network repeatedly linked Father Ignacio Ellacuría and his colleagues to the FMLN, and demanded his extermination. Now you acknowledge having authorized the raid, the purpose of which was to gather the necessary information to execute the military operation of the massacre. These acts, the links and your conduct involve you as a suspect, at least in the cover-up of the crime."

3. Confidence in you as an interlocutor in the dialogue and negotiation process has seriously deteriorated due to your own behavior. Your credibility has collapsed and this can irreparably damage the process toward a political solution and peace."

"You are obliged to cooperate with the court without reservations in the prompt resolution of the crime of the Jesuit priests and to make public absolutely everything you know; you must explain convincingly your own responsibility in the decisions and orders related to the case."

"In this way you would make an important contribution to justice and the achievement of peace in our suffering country."

"This is an unavoidable obligation for you."

"In any democratic country your resignation and those of the High Command would have been requested."

—FMLN General Command, July 26, 1990

7/27 President Cristiani holds a press conference at mid-day:

Jesuit Investigation: "The FMLN letter is a smoke screen . . . I am always at the disposition of the court . . . I haven't hidden anything . . . I have explained that raids must be ordered by the High Command and authorized . . . There were various requests for raids during the offensive . . . The High Command, in my presence, gave the order . . . I authorized it, I did not order it directly . . . This letter is part of their strategy . . . It doesn't bother me because I feel free of anything." (Sonora)

7/27 Lt. Col. Carlos Camilo Hérnandez appears in court this morning to present his testimony on the destruction of the log books from the Military School. As he leaves the courthouse, Hérnandez tells reporters he expects to be released on bail next week. "I gave my statement and now it's clear that I haven't committed any crime. They're talking about my release and the picture looks better." (TV 6, 12, Sonora) A U.S. military officer and a member of the Embassy staff were seen in the courthouse today. (DL) Judge Zamora has not yet responded to request from the defense for a change of venue to Santa Tecla. (TV 6) Eduardo Pineda of the Attorney General's office says a change of venue would "set back" the case. (DH 7/28)

7/31 In a telephone interview today, Ana Guadalupe Mártinez says the amnesty proposal supported by Colonel Ponce is a "smoke screen . . . He should clean up his own house first. He should put himself at the disposition of the courts in the Jesuit case . . . and be an example of commitment and responsibility to the San José Agreement." (Horizonte)

7/31 A member of the prosecution team in the Jesuit case says the change of venue appeal could be a serious setback, "just as the case is reaching a difficult stage." (DH)

7/31 Lt. Col. Camilo Hérnandez released on 30,000 colón bail today. (DL) His defense attorney says no one has proved a crime was committed. "There was no important information in the books." (TV 12)

August 1990

8/1 Jesuit case will continue after the August holidays; court official says Judge Zamora will respond to the change of venue petition "in due time"; the two North American officers and two Salvadoran colonels expected to testify sometime after August 8th. (TV 12) Over one hundred witnesses have testified to date. (DL) The U.S. government has not yet responded to the judge's request to subpoena Major Eric Buckland and Colonel Menjivar.

8/2 PDC leader Gerardo LeChevalier questions the "silence" of President Cristiani about his responsibility for the raid on the Jesuit house, November 13. "Surprisingly, overnight, the news was dropped like a bomb, and not even the judge has asked what had happened and why this information was hidden." Several weeks ago the President admitted he had "authorized" the raid. (DL)

8/6 "The most important achievement of the judicial system so far in the investigation is that it has demonstrated that most members of the Armed Forces to not want to collaborate," says Jesuit Provincial Tojeira. "The defense is immoral. They say there is no evidence against Benavides and the others, but there is sufficient evidence to take the case to trial. We are not against a pardon, but we are after truth and justice." (TV 12)

8/7 The Jesuit case could be set back at least two months if Judge Zamora denies the change of venue petition and the defense appeals. According to court officials, the Foreign Ministry has still not received a response to the subpoena request for Major Eric Buckland. (EM)

8/7 U.S. Embassy notifies the press that a delegation representing the Moakley Task Force is in the country until August 10th. (TV 12)

8/8 Moakley delegation meets with Judge Ricardo Zamora and with UCA officials. (TV 6, 12)

8/8 Judge Zamora subpoenas an employee of the Military School, Nelson Arnoldo Lazo, a file clerk. Lazo is scheduled to testify August 10th. (TV 6)

8/9 PDC leader Eduardo Colíndres says President Cristiani must "tell all he knows" about the Jesuit case. "As Commander-in-Chief he must know everything and he must tell the truth. If not, he is leaving room for doubts about the degree of his participation." (DL)

8/9 Defense Attorney for the military in the Jesuit case, José Raúl Méndez Castro, says the legal process "is not valid" because it is based on the investigation conducted by the Special Investigation Unit (SIU), "which is an auxiliary organ, not a legal entity," and because statements were taken from the accused more than 72 hours after their detention. "The prosecution cannot continue. At the end the case will be dismissed for lack of legal evidence." He confirms that the defense will appeal if Judge Zamora denies the change of venue petition. (EM)

8/9 Judge Zamora has received notice from the Foreign Ministry that the U.S. government will not permit Major Buckland to testify. The statement from the Embassy reads, "U.S. military advisors enjoy the same legal status, privileges and exemptions as technical personnel of the Embassy, Consular and security personnel, according to an agreement between the military forces of both countries signed in 1988. Major Buckland is not subject to Salvadoran law and can refuse to appear, based on Article 31 of the Vienna Convention on Diplomatic Relations." (LPG 8/10) Judge Zamora will request the assistance of the Supreme Court. (TV 6)

8/9 Moakley delegation "concerned" about eventual set back in the Jesuit case. (DH)

8/10 Moakley delegation meets with the Inter-Party Commission to discuss progress in the negotiations; ARENA does not participate in the meeting. According to Mario Aguiñada Carranza, party leaders informed the delegation that participation of opposition parties in the next election will be "evaluated," depending on the results of the negotiations toward demilitarization. ARENA has not participated in consensus decisions in the elections, human rights or administration of justice sub-commissions. "No substantive agreements have been reached," says Carranza. "The process is extremely difficult. We hope the Moakley Commission will contribute to the negotiation process, as they have to the Jesuit investigation." (Sonora, Horizonte)

8/10 Nelson Arnoldo Lazo, employee of the Military School, ignores second subpoena from Judge Zamora to testify in the Jesuit case and could be arrested for failure to appear. Lazo's responsibility during the offensive was to check in weapons as troops returned from missions. (LPG 8/11)

8/11 Sources close to the Jesuit investigation charge that the State Department has twenty-one secret documents related to the case but refuses to release them "for reasons of national security." Embassy spokesperson Jeff Brown denies the charge and says the US is "sharing all information that will contribute to the case." The charges were made by Father Pedro Armada, of the Jesuit Office on Central America. (TV12)

8/13 Attorney General Mendoza confirms denial of the change of venue appeal in the Jesuit case.

8/14 Nelson Rivas Lazo, employee of the Military School subpoenaed twice by Judge Zamora, "hasn't worked there since December 31st," according to information received this week by the court. (DH)

8/14 Yesterday a lieutenant from the Military School testified in court and denied any AK-47s were on the premises in November. Today a member of the prosecution team says, "The witness lied. There were AK-47s in the School. The High Command has acknowledged the existence of the AK-47 that killed two of the priests and Colonel Hérnandez

said the weapons were there "for study . . . draw your own conclusions."
(TV 12)

8/14   Attorney General Mendoza says the investigation is "going
well—slow but sure." North Americans Major Eric Buckland and Colonel
Menjivar are "key witnesses for the prosecution." (EM)

8/14   The Moakley Report is "pure speculation," says Defense Attorney Méndez. "We are in a legal process based on our laws. We must
define the trial. Anything else is speculation. If there is no evidence
against our clients, it is correct that they be released." (EM)

8/15   "The United States is not exerting sufficient pressure to resolve
the case," says Jesuit priest Fermín Saenz. "The State Department must
take an active position, not just observe. Many people must know what
happened, including the Embassy and the CIA . . . If the will had existed,
the case could have been solved in a week. The crime itself was very
complicated.   Whoever received the order received very clear instructions. There is a systematic effort to block the investigation on the
part of the military. A lot is lacking in order to break the barriers." (TV
12)

8/15   In Washington, Congressman Joe Moakley issues a statement on
the case: "I believe that the High Command of the Salvadoran Armed
Forces is engaged in a conspiracy to obstruct justice in the Jesuit case.
Salvadoran military officers have withheld evidence, destroyed evidence,
falsified evidence and repeatedly perjured themselves in testimony before
the judge. I do not believe this could be done without at least the tacit
consent of the High Command."

"Even more important, I believe the High Command's goal, from the
beginning, has been to control the investigation and to limit the number
and rank of the officers who will be held responsible for the crimes. As a
result, some individuals who may have direct knowledge of the murders
have been shielded from serious investigation."

"Because of this, progress in the case remains slow. This is true de-
spite the courage and initiative of the man in charge of the investigation,
Judge Ricardo Zamora, and despite the urgings of Salvadoran President,
Alfredo Cristiani, and U.S. Ambassador to El Salvador, William Walker."

"I am encouraged, however, that many members of the Armed Forces who were not involved in the crimes are angered at the possibility that U.S. military aid will be reduced because of the actions of the High Command. As a result, the Armed Forces are increasingly divided, and pressure is growing for an end to the conspiracy of silence and lies that . . . from day one has characterized the military's attitude toward this case." (Press Release)

8/15 Two FBI agents are in the country examining Colonel Benavides' order book; results should be known next week. (TV 12)

8/16 According to the testimony of Lt. Francisco Gallardo Mata in the Jesuit case last week, he did not turn over weapons to or receive them from members of the Atlacatl Battalion. He said he knew two of the accused, Espinoza Guerra and Yusshy Mendoza but "didn't remember seeing them on November 15-16" and "didn't remember anyone leaving the Military School on those dates." (DH)

8/17 Eight members of the Moakley delegation in the country last week visited Colonel Benavides on August 10th, accompanied by Colonel Wheeler of the U.S. Military Group. (LPG)

8/17 Judge Zamora sent a questionnaire to Colonel Ponce to return to the court; Ponce's first statement was December 11th. (DH)

8/17 Colonel Vargas "totally rejects" charges by Congressmember Moakley that the military is blocking the investigation. (Horizonte)

8/17 Ministry of Defense responds to statement by Congressmember Moakley, calling his accusations, "speculation" and "totally false . . . The Armed Forces has cooperated in total honesty with the Judge. The Minister of Defense and the High Command have responded rapidly to all requests. The comments are of a political nature and have no legal basis. It is an attempt to discredit the Armed Forces. There is no division and no conspiracy of silence. The Armed Forces is committed to a resolution of the unfortunate incident. Mr. Moakley's conclusions question Salvadoran law and can harm the position of the government in the negotiations." (Horizonte)

8/17 Presidential Aide Ernesto Altschul also criticizes the report and says, "it is not an official document, just a press release. Anyone who has evidence should present it to Judge Zamora." (TV 12)

8/17 Guillermo Ungo says the press release from Congressmember Moakley gave "breathing room" to President Cristiani. "They are trying to save him but he is the Commander-in-Chief. He is responsible. This gives him space to rectify his position." (TV 12)

8/17 The Moakley charges were "mistaken," says Colonel Elena Fuentes. "We have our own laws. These are just speculations, intervening in our internal affairs." Elena Fuentes is "optimistic" about dialogue, but says the participation of social forces is incorrect. "Everyone wants to get their hands in it, which is not convenient." (TV 12)

8/18 FMLN releases a letter to President Cristiani proposing the formation of a joint FMLN-government commission to oversee the investigation of the Jesuit case. "Nine months after the crime nothing has been resolved, confirming that impunity continues." The letter suggests the President must clarify his own knowledge of the case and that Colonel Ponce should be prosecuted, "not promoted to Minister of Defense." (TV 12) The amnesty proposal, "forgive and forget," is "a cover-up for horrendous crimes." (Horizonte)

8/18 José María López of the Political/Diplomatic Commission of the FMLN says that comments by Colonel Vargas and the Ministry of Defense about the Moakley statement "demonstrate that impunity continues to exist." (Horizonte)

8/18 Prosecuting Attorney Sidney Blanco says "high-ranking officers are covering-up the Jesuit case. We don't know exactly who they are. None of the witnesses who have testified have told the truth. All of them have lied in one way or another, but even from the lies some other information can be obtained." (Horizontte)

8/18 The Moakley Report "confirms the need to demilitarize the country," says Rubén Zamora. "It confirms what we all know about impunity. The Armed Forces and government are in a dead-end street, as a result of their own actions. The judicial system suffers more than any other institution in the country from militarism and impunity. The changes that are being made, the Office of Information on Detained Persons, for example, are good but not enough. It's like giving aspirin to a dying cancer patient. It must be reformed from top to bottom along with demilitarization." (TV 12)

8/20 President Cristiani, the President of the Supreme Court, Minister of Defense, Chief of Staff of the Armed Forces, Vice-Ministers of Defense and Public Security meet with Judge Zamora for four hours this morning to discuss the Jesuit case. (TV 12)

8/21 Jesuit Provincial José María Tojeira says three other colonels could be involved in the case, "a small group of colonels of higher rank than Benavides." Tojeira names Colonels Cerna Flores, Guzmán Aguilar and Linares. Cerna Flores and Guzmán Aguilar were suddenly transferred to other positions after the offensive; Linares, former head of the Atlacatl Battalion was recently transferred to Military Detachment #4 in Morazan. (TV 12) Joaquin Cerna Flores was chief of operations during the offensive; was transferred to ANTEL on January 3rd. Guzmán Aguilar was head of the National Police until October, then transferred to the National Intelligence Department (DNI) and appointed Military Attaché to Costa Rica in January. None of the officers have been questioned about the case.

8/21 Judge Zamora has subpoenaed members of the Atlacatl Battalion to testify August 22 and 24. (LPG)

8/22 U.S. Ambassador William Walker says the FMLN proposal to demobilize the army is "absurd." "The existence of the Armed Forces as an institution is untouchable." A reduction of troops could be "positive in the eyes of the U.S.," he says. "Everyone is talking about the role of the Armed Forces in a democratic society. This is important." (Horizonte)

On the Jesuit case, Walker suggests Jesuit José María Tojeira "talk to Judge Zamora," and says, "We have to come to the end of this process. It is harmful to the country and to the Armed Forces but it must continue to the end." (TV 12)

8/22 Merino also criticizes José María Tojeira saying the Jesuits should not make public accusations. Colonel Guzmán Aguilar was "out of the country" during the offensive, says Merino. "I don't know how he came to this conclusion." (TV 12) "If he has evidence, it should be presented." (DL)

8/22 Colonel Joaquin Cerna Flores says he has "no opinion" about accusations made by Jesuit Tojeira but he is available if called by the judge. No one from the High Command is available to discuss the issue with the press. (TV 12)

8/22 Sidney Blanco of the prosecution team says Tojeira's statement was "a result of his analysis. Any person who examined the case would come to the same conclusion. This is not new for us. We aren't surprised, he is right. It is a logical conclusion." (TV 12)

8/22 "The court must call them to testify," says a defense attorney in the Jesuit case. "They should testify in person. Written statements are too bureaucratic and we believe privileged witnesses should renounce that right." (TV 12)

8/23 José María Tojeira interviewed on "Buenos Días" this morning. He repeats his accusations against the three colonels, insisting that they must be investigated. "This is a friendly effort to collaborate with the military," he says, "they must make their own investigation." The Jesuit Provincial is pleased with the meeting between Cristiani, the High Command and Judge Zamora. "It was a recognition for Zamora. He has been courageous and honest throughout this process. This gives him more weight and protection." Tojeira believes Cristiani, Ponce and Larios have shown "good will" in the investigation. "If the High Command doesn't like the Moakley report, they need to make a serious internal investigation." Documents have been requested from U.S. agencies and the State Department, but, according to Tojeira, the DIA refused, citing "national security." The National Security Council "said they had a lot but could only send us newspaper clippings," and the State Department sent information from the Embassy. Asked about his own security, Tojeira replies, "It's a risk but one has to live with risks in a country at war. I don't think anyone wants to continue killing priests." (TV 12)

8/23 Judge Zamora will subpoena the three colonels, Guzmán Aguilar, Cerna Flores and Linares in the coming weeks. (TV 12) Two soldiers of the Atlacatl Battalion, First Sergeant Oscar Armando Solorzano Esquivel and Sgt. Rafael Molina Aguilar expected to testify tomorrow. (LPG)

8/23 Rubén Zamora believes U.S. advisors were involved in the Jesuit assassinations. "For this reason there hasn't been much pressure from the U.S. The pressure that has come has been from Congress. The U.S. is in an awkward situation. If the investigation goes all the way it will uncover U.S. advisors. They are covering up for the Armed Forces in order to cover-up for themselves." (TV 12)

8/23 Francisco Mena Sandoval, former Armed Forces captain, now FMLN Commander, says the death of the Jesuits is an institutional problem. "It wasn't just a bullet that escaped from a soldier or a colonel. It was an error that is going to cost the Armed Forces strategically, a cost that they cannot pay because here it is important to point out that what the Armed Forces did with the Jesuits, they do daily in El Salvador against *campesinos*, workers, students, professionals. But with the Jesuits, the procedures of the Armed Forces have come to light so now the people know clearly. Even the North Americans are clear that they have created a monster they cannot control."

8/24 Judge Ricardo Zamora denies change of venue petition in the Jesuit case, arguing the conspiracy occurred in the Military School, jurisdiction of San Salvador. (Horizonte)

8/24 Two soldiers of the Atlacatl Battalion are scheduled to appear in court to testify in the Jesuit Case; the two participated in the raid of the Jesuit house on November 13 and in the military operation of the 16th.

First Sergeant Oscar Armando Solórzano Esquivel gives contradictory testimony, according to Prosecuting Attorney Sidney Blanco. Judge Zamora orders his arrest, but soldiers refuse to carry out the order. "He refused to recognize a photo of himself," says Blanco. Zamora has also asked Minister of Defense Larios to send a list of all officers who participated in the staff meeting on the night of November 15. (TV 6, 12) Sgt. Molina Aguilar was reported as "very nervous. He asked to be excused to vomit." The "incredible escape" occurs as Zamora tells the National Guard to hold Solórzano while the arrest warrant is written; apparently a defense attorney tells the sergeants and their guards that the order is illegal and they flee. (EM)

8/25 The Atlacatl sergeant who escaped from the courthouse yesterday will be detained, according to a statement from the Armed Forces. (TV 12)

8/26 Lt. Col. Camilo Hérnandez, former Assistant Director of the Military School, accused of destroying evidence in the Jesuit case, is reported wounded during combat at Cerron Grande near San José Las Flores, Chalatenango. (Horizonte) Hérnandez, now Executive officer of the Belloso Battalion, was apparently wounded by a mine at midnight last night. (LPG 8/27)

8/26 Bishop Rosa Chávez cites the case of Sergeant Solórzano fleeing from the courthouse. "The image of this man running from his responsibility is the image of the Armed Forces running from the truth." (TV 12)

8/27 Sgt. Oscar Solórzano will reportedly be turned over to the court this morning. (LPG

8/27 The Jesuit investigation is "80% complete," according to the President of the Supreme Court. (EM)

8/27 Sergeant Oscar Solórzano of the Atlacatl Battalion is brought to court this afternoon by two National Police agents in civilian clothes. (Horizonte) Solórzano declines to testify, saying he is ill. (TV 12)

8/28 Yesterday the defense in the Jesuit case filed an appeal to reverse Judge Zamora's denial of the change of venue petition. If the appeals court accepts the petition, the case could be set back at least two months, according to a court official who says, important procedures and declarations need to be completed including the reconstruction of the crime and testimonies of Major Buckland and the three colonels named by Tojeira. (EM) "The case could be in suspense for months." (TV 12)

8/28 Judge Zamora sets 15,000 colón embargo on property of Sergeant Oscar Solórzano, 29 after he appears in court again and denies all charges. (Horizonte) Solórzano could receive 1 to 5 years for false testimony. (TV 12)

8/28 Another article in *El Mundo* says the Minister of Defense could be Ponce, Rubio or Vargas, "but the position does not necessarily have to be filled by an active-duty military officer. It could be a civilian with political, military and administrative experience. There is no requirement that he be military, much less that he be a general." This source also says, "We have to recognize that Ponce has a problem with the Jesuit case." (EM) Colonel Sigifredo Ochóa Pérez would fit the description of a person with political/military/administrative experience.

8/28 Former Captain Francisco Mena Sandoval, now FMLN military advisor, is interviewed by phone from Mexico. He says the purging of officers is nothing new, 44 colonels and generals were expelled in 1970. "Our historic error was that we left five colonels." The Jesuit case will be blocked, according to Mena Sandoval, "as long as the Armed Forces does not make a decision to take responsibility. It is Cristiani's responsibility to clean-up the institution."

8/28 PADECOES announces the repopulation of La Joya, Morazan on August 31st; the community will be renamed "Comunidad Martín Baró," in honor of the Jesuit slain in November. (Horizonte) There are fifteen repopulations in the country, with 29,000 inhabitants.

8/29 Appeals Court denies change of venue appeal in the Jesuit case, "in record time," ruling the arguments are "not applicable . . . Only the Supreme Court can resolve the conflict according to the Constitution." (TV 12)

8/29 Judge Zamora receives a North American delegation representing the firm of Saperstein, Seligman and Mayeda. (DH 8/30)

8/30 Minister of Defense Larios has sent a list of all commanders present at the meeting on the night of November 15, but will be requested again to provide information on the discussion that occurred. (EM)

8/30 According to Sergeant Oscar Solórzano's testimony last week, he "doesn't remember" participating in the reconstruction of the crime conducted by the SIC, he "doesn't remember" if he was photographed and "doesn't know" any of the officers or fellow soldiers of his unit who participated in the raid on the Jesuit house November 13. (EM) He stated that he arrived at the Military School on the afternoon of November 13, under the orders of Lt. Espinoza; the raid was carried out "in a place he doesn't know the name of." He "didn't see anyone there except the Atlacatl soldiers." He returned to the Military School and "never left" on the day of the 15th of November. On the morning of the 16th he joined other Atlacatl troops in Zacamil. Solórzano said he was "pressured" by the SIC, "forced to sign a document without reading it," and he "doesn't know" which Atlacatl soldiers were involved in the assassinations. (DL)

September 1990

9/1 Gutierrez Castro also says there have been "notable advances" in the case and "all evidence points to Colonel Benavides." (Sonora)

9/1 A member of the prosecution team says there are "no more possibilities" of setbacks in the Jesuit investigation; the defense has exhausted the appeals process on the change of venue petition. (TV 12)

9/1 At 1:00 am this morning National Police and Municipal Police round up seventy street vendors who occupy posts in the Plaza Civica, arrest them and confiscate their goods. UDN charges the arrests were ordered by Mayor Calderón Sol to "clean up" the Plaza before today's ceremonies with the President. (Horizonte) Cristiani says "peace is the primary objective of our government. We must put aside egoism and hatred and build a monument to peace and solidarity in our hearts." (TV12)

9/2 It is not clear if the government economic program can resolve the crisis, says Archbishop Rivera. "In recent months the government has recognized that the majority of Salvadorans live in extreme poverty and cannot even meet basic needs. The drama of unemployment is also distressing. It is not clear if the path proposed by the government is really the most adequate to resolve the problems of the poor." After Mass the Archbishop says that the appointment of a civilian Minister of Defense "would have been an important step in the process of demilitarization" but "we believe that the new Minister is going to be interested in the dialogue and a resolution to the Jesuit case." (EM, TV 12, 9/3) The previous military tanda in power had better communication with the Church than the Tandona but "the hope exists that once again an understanding military hierarchy will return." He criticizes the campaign against the popular organizations saying, "I believe humanitarian organizations must be respected. This type of campaign doesn't contribute anything to peace." (DL 9/3)

9/3 Colonel René Emilio Ponce sworn in as Minister of Defense; promises total support and collaboration with Judge Zamora in the Jesuit case and says, "If all the commanders must testify to clear up this case, all will do it, as many times as necessary." (TV 6, LPG 9/4)

9/3 Two soldiers of the Atlacatl Battalion testify in court today, Héctor Antonio Guerrero Maravilla and Rufino Barrientos Ramos. (LPG 9/4) Judge Zamora received the written, notarized statements of Larios and Ponce last week. (TV 12)

9/5 The collaboration of the military in the Jesuit case is "more serious and efficient now," according to the President of the Supreme Court. He says the investigation will not be affected by the negotiations. "We will not accept any conditions." (TV 12)

9/5 In Washington, Ambassador Salaverria says the Jesuit assassination should not affect U.S. aid. "This is the broadest investigation in the history of El Salvador." (TV 12)

9/5 In his testimony last week, General Larios swore the UCA was not discussed during the meeting of 24 commanders on November 15. The meeting lasted from 6-10:00 pm . . . President Cristiani arrived at 11:00 p.m. according to Larios, and left at 2:00 am on November 16 after authorizing all operations. The court also reports that accused Lt. Gonzalo Guervara Cerritos is suffering eye ailments and will receive medical treatment. (DH)

9/5 In Colonel Ponce's sworn statement he said Colonels Avilés, López y López and Rivas all denied making any comments about the participation of Colonel Benavides in the Jesuit massacre. He stated that military security in Colonias Arce and Palmera was beefed up on November 13 and a Security Command formed for the Military Complex. The Colonel also mentioned receiving a report from the National Police on the 15th of November that union leaders would meet in the UCA. (EM) Ponce said that Colonel Milton Menjívar of the US Milgroup informed him on January 2 of the accusations against Benavides; the same day he met with Buckland and Avilés and later with Colonel López y López. Both colonels denied Buckland's statement. (LPG 9/6) Ponce authorized the search of the Jesuit house at 8:40 pm, according to his statement; the raid occurred at 6:30 pm. (LPG 9/6)

9/6 Ex-Jesuit priest Ricardo de la Cierva, Spaniard, accused Ignacio Ellacuría of being a "strategist of Marxism" in an article, "The Secret of Ellacuría," published in the Spanish journal "Epoca." *Diario De Hoy* publishes a summary, saying de la Cierva believed it was his "duty to reveal the link between Ellacuría and the Marxist left." (DH)

9/7 Judge Zamora orders provisional detention of the two Atlacatl soldiers who testified last week, bringing the total number of detainees to twelve. Héctor Antonio Guerrero, 25, and Rufino Barrientos Ramos, 23, are charged with giving false testimony. (EM, Horizonte)

9/7 President Cristiani appears in court today in the late afternoon to testify in the Jesuit case. (Sonora)

9/10 According to President Cristiani's testimony in court on September 7, he received a call from General Larios between 10:30 and 11:00 pm on the night of November 15 and came immediately to the High Command with Antonio Tona because he was residing in his home during the offensive. He was told it was necessary to push the "terrorists" out of Cerro El Carmen and Las Colinas, north of Mejicanos and the use of tanks and artillery was proposed, "because the civilians had been evacuated." The UCA was never discussed according to the President. He then went to the Tactical Operations Center; 2-3 U.S. advisors were present but he did not talk with them. He returned to the residence at 2:30 a.m . . . (LPG) The President met with Ponce, Larios, Montano and Zépeda "who had analyzed the military situation and said it was necessary to change the security plan for the area to the north of the capital, 'the command post of the FMLN.'" (Horizonte) An official of the prosecutor's office says it is "unfortunate" that the President came to the court after court hours on the 7th because no one was there to interview him, just an assistant. The Judge was not advised beforehand of the President's appearance. (TV 12)

9/10 Today, Major Mauricio Chávez Caceres of COPREFA and Colonel Juan Emilio Velásquez Alfaro of the Bracamonte Battalion appear in court to present testimonies. Both agree that the UCA was not discussed on the night of November 15 and Chávez Caceres insists that COPREFA never released any information on the crime or accused the FMLN. He says C5 of the High Command (Colonel Avilés) was "responsible for the campaign against the Jesuits." (Horizonte, TV 12)

9/11 Colonel Zépeda scheduled to appear in court today. (YSU)

9/11 Prosecuting attorney says new contradictions arose during yesterday's testimonies: Benavides was not in command of the area in December as had been stated previously but was replaced on December 1st. (TV 12) And COPREFA was not responsible for Radio Cuscatlán: Mauricio Sandoval (National Secretary of Information, responsible to the President) and C5 of the High Command (Colonel Avilés) were responsible. (TV 12)

9/12 In Washington, Jesuit Jon Cortina calls for an end to military aid in a press conference attended by Senators John Kerry and Brock Adams. Cortina describes army actions against the community "Ignacio Ellacuría" August 21-25, which he says were witnessed by International Red Cross personnel. Cortina was the target of a sniper attack during that operation and says he received "multiple death threats" during a two-week period. (DL)

9/12 According to the testimony of Major Chávez Caceres of COPREFA, he heard the news about the Jesuit killings on the radio. He also said that he met with Mauricio Sandoval and Colonel Avilés and suggested the open microphones on Radio Cuscatlán were "not convenient." (LPG) COPREFA had "no jurisdiction" over Radio Cuscatlán and Chávez Caceres said he "didn't know" if C5 (military psychological warfare department) placed messages on the radio, "because he never listened to it." (DL)

9/12 Colonel Juan Vicente Equizabal, Executive Officer of the National Guard testifies in the Jesuit case today. (EM) Lt. Colonel Velasco Alfaro also appears; he was named head of the security command of the Military Complex early in December, to replace Colonel Benavides. He says he was in the meeting on November 15, but "doesn't remember" if the UCA was discussed or if foreigners or civilians were in the meeting. (LPG, EM 9/13)

9/13 During first day of fifth round of negotiations in San José, discussion focuses on three points raised by the FMLN: freedom of the press, the formation of a joint commission to follow the Jesuit investigation and a complete investigation of the Romero assassination including release of information retained by the DNI on the case. (Horizonte)

9/14 Colonels Héctor Heriberto Hérnandez and Ivan López y López testify today in the Jesuit case; all statements of high-level military officers will be taken in the building of the Supreme Court as the result of an agreement between the Judge and the military, "for better security." The 24 officers who participated in the November 15 meeting have been subpoenaed. (Horizonte)

9/16 In Spain, Jesuit Jon Sobrino says the investigation is not moving ahead. "The U.S. is not collaborating." He calls for the purification of the Armed Forces. (Horizonte)

9/16 Archbishop Rivera y Damas during Sunday homily says he is "uncomfortable" with the U.S. policy on the Jesuits and fears that the aid will not be cut, "using the argument of another offensive" and the investigation will not continue . . . (DL)

9/17 Henry Campos of the Attorney General's office says the testimony of military officers "has complicated the case. They are not aiding the investigation. They are not providing any new information. They are coming to ratify some points already made, nothing new. But it is important that they have renounced their immunity privileges." (Horizonte)

9/18 During Colonel Héctor Heriberto Hérnandez's testimony last week he claimed the Treasury Police found weapons in the UCA "just before the offensive," but he "doesn't remember the date" and "can't specify the quantity or quality." He said he ordered the search, and the weapons were found in the patio. He also "doesn't remember" if the UCA was discussed at the meeting on November 15. (DH)

9/18 "It is totally false," responds Jesuit Rogelio Pedraz. (Horizonte) "He doesn't know when or what he found. I would think a truly capable army would have a record of this. If this gentleman doesn't remember any more it is not worth wasting words." (TV 12)

9/18 Colonel Ivan López y López said he was an advisor to Colonel Rivas of the SIC during the early part of the investigation, because he formerly headed the commission. He "doesn't remember" if SIC had a list of possible suspects and says a meeting of union leaders in the UCA on the night of November 15 was not discussed at the High Command meeting the same night. (EM)

9/18 Colonel Zépeda to court today. (Horizonte)

9/19 A coalition of religious and pacifist groups in the U.S. begins a strong lobby campaign to end aid, including radio and television spots with images of the Jesuit assassinations and the four North American churchworkers assassinated in 1980. (TV 12)

9/19 In Colonel Zépeda's testimony yesterday he denied that the Jesuit massacre was planned in advance and said that Benavides was responsible, "because he was responsible for the zone." (TV 6) "Benavides received orders via C3 of the High Command whose chief in November was Colonel Joaquin Cerna Flores, who in turn was under the responsibility of Colonel Ponce." (LPG 9/20)

9/20 Jesuits deny statement by Colonel Hérnandez of a raid and weapons in the UCA before the offensive. Fermin Saenz says a military patrol came to the UCA on November 12, the second day of the offensive, with an alleged guerrilla tied up and found some military equipment outside the gate. (Horizonte)

9/21 Colonels Joaquin Cerna Flores and Roberto Esteban Santos testify today in the Jesuit case. (Sonora) Esteban Santos is identified as "an engineer working for the state." (EM) Cerna Flores testifies for seven hours. Defense attorney says the process is "coming to a conclusion." (TV 12)

9/21 U.S. Senators Charles Robb and John McCain in the country to meet with the President, Minister of Defense, High Command and Judge Zamora. (EM)

9/21 Foreign Minister Pacas Castro returns from tour of Latin America, Europe and Washington; says the Jesuit case is the main concern in the U.S. "I repeated the commitment of the government to continue the process." (TV 6)

9/24 Colonel Joaquin Cerna Flores, head of operations for the military during the offensive and currently Director General of ANTEL tells the press that he ordered the search of the Jesuit house on November 13 because he "had information of guerrilla presence" but says the raid "was not linked to the assassinations." He insists his post was "administrative". "I only transmitted the order for the raid." (Horizonte)

9/24 Colonel Montano repeats statement by Colonel Héctor Heriberto Hérnandez that there was a raid in the Loyola Center of the UCA and that weapons were found. "I am not accusing the Church but we have the documentation and the captured materials." (TV 12)

9/24 Lt. Nelson Alberto Barra testifies today from 8:30-11:30 am . . . Described as a "collaborator" of Colonel Benavides in the Military School during the offensive, Barra is currently serving in the Artillery Brigade. (DL) He says he is only aware of Atlacatl soldiers leaving the Military School at 5:00 am on November 16 and "doesn't know" of any movement earlier during the night. (TV 12)

9/24 Lt. Ricardo Gallardo Mata was subpoenaed to appear today but does not show. (TV 12)

9/25 In Washington, President Cristiani has breakfast with Congress members Dave McCurdy and Joe Moakley, then a private meeting with Moakley; also meets with the Foreign Relations Committee, Foreign Affairs Committee, George Mitchell and Cristopher Dodd. (TV 12) Cristiani says he is "willing" to ask "noted jurists" to assist with the Jesuit investigation. (Horizonte)

9/25 Jesuit Fermin Saenz, Director of the Loyola Center on the UCA campus submitted a statement to Judge Zamora on an unspecified date saying that during the afternoon and evening of November 15 personnel of the Center served coffee and sweet rolls to a company of the Atlacatl Battalion that was camped out on the property of the Center. On November 15, according to the statement, approximately 130 soldiers of the Atlacatl were in the area. "After talking with several of their commanders we offered sweet rolls and coffee and more than 80 of them ate. In the evening the troops left heading in the direction of Jardines de Guadalupe, hours before the massacre." (EM)

9/25 Captain Julio Armando Garcia Oliva and José Heriberto Valle testify in court this morning. Garcia Oliva commanded units of Military Detachments 6 and 7 in the zone of the UCA during the offensive and testified previously on July 4. José Heriberto Valle was the personal assistant to Lt. Yusshy Mendoza, one of the officers detained for the crime. Both testify that "nothing abnormal" occurred during the night of the 15-16 of November. (LPG 9/26) Valle says he "slept in the corridor" next to the room of Lt. Mendoza who "never left all night." Prosecuting attorney Henry Campos declines to comment on the testimonies. "It would not be convenient to say what our opinion is. We do have an opinion about the truth but can't give it right now." (TV 12) Garcia verifies gunfire near the UCA on the morning of November 16 and that "it was not an encounter with the terrorists." He says Lt. Gallardo Mata headed a unit of soldiers from DM#6 who were positioned near the Colonial Theater right behind the UCA; at 2:00 am there was combat in Antiguo Cuscatlán and two soldiers wounded but also simultaneous shots and explosions during a twenty-minute period near the UCA. According to Garcia, Lt. Gallardo Mata confirmed to him that the shooting was not the result of combat. (DH 9/27)

9/25 According to the testimony of Colonel Joaquin Cerna Flores last week, he ordered the search on November 13 as head of C3 (Operations) but it was unrelated to the assassinations. "Colonel Ponce and I chose the commandos of the Atlacatl Battalion to search the UCA on November 13. In the afternoon we had received telephone calls from civilians and reports from Intelligence of the presence of subversives inside the UCA."

At 7:00 pm two officers, whose names he "doesn't remember" came to inform him that they arrived in the capital with a unit of the Atlacatl and were sent to the Military School to integrate into the Security Command.

"At 8:00 pm Colonel Ponce ordered me to order the search of the UCA and after a brief discussion we concluded the most appropriate unit was the Atlacatl." Cerrna Flores says he immediately called the officer in command and ordered the search but he did not inform Colonel Benavides of the order because "he determined that the officers of the Atlacatl would present the report."

"At 10:30 pm the officer who led the search reported on the results saying there was no presence of subversives and that they had been attended by a priest they believed to be Ignacio Ellacuría."

Cerna Flores says he participated in the meeting on November 15 in the High Command, then went to the Joint Operations Center and didn't meet with anyone else. He learned about the crime at 9:00 am "on the radio." (LPG 9/26) Note: The search of the UCA took place around 6:30 pm.

Cerna Flores also states that the Atlacatl was the only unit that received orders to carry out the search and he "doesn't know" how an official of the DNI was there . . . "and it is not usual that an officer of DNI would observe a search, especially when it is carried out by an infantry unit."

The Atlacatl unit left the morning of the 16th for Zacamil, according to Cerna, because Lt. Col. León Linares had been asking him by radio since the 14th to send the commandos to Zacamil.

Colonel Ponce appointed Benavides head of the Security Command; Cerna says he was not responsible for Benavides nor does he know if the High Command named any officers to participate in the commando unit. "The Security Command depended on the senior officer of the Joint High Command in operative aspects and had under its orders the Atlacatl unit, a unit of the Libertadores of the Treasury Police, two companies of the Training Center of Immediate Reaction Battalions (CEBRI), a battalion of the Cazadores of Sonsonate, an artillery unit, a cavalry unit and small units of the Military and National Police." The CEAT (Special Anti-Terrorist Command of the Treasury Police) was not under operational jurisdiction of the Security Command nor under orders of the Joint High

Command until November 16, when it was placed under the jurisdiction of the High Command; "before November 16, it was under the operational jurisdiction of the Director, Colonel Héctor Heriberto Hérnandez . . . "

"The fact that armed subjects had entered the UCA to assassinate the Jesuits, and the possibility of modifying the security displacement in this sector was not the responsibility of C3, but of the head of the Security Command. The person in charge of calling on Colonel Benavides in respect to the error in the security displacement was the Chief of the High Command." (DL 9/26)

9/26 Colonel Elmer Francisco Roque testifies in the Fourth Court today. He is responsible for finances for the High Command; was subpoenaed because he was present in the meeting on the night of November 15. (TV 6)

9/26 Colonel Oscar Len Linares, Commander of the Atlacatl during the offensive, testifies today in the Supreme Court building. (Horizonte)

9/26 "Eighty percent of the testimonies of military officers contradict each other," says a prosecuting attorney, "which leads us to believe something is being hidden." The prosecution will make the contradictions public in the near future. Since Cristiani's appearance in court, all twenty-four officers present at the meeting on November 15 have been subpoenaed but "none have provided information on the intellectual authors of the crime." Eduardo Pineda says "related sectors must assist." (Horizonte) Pineda also rejects Cristiani's proposal to bring U.S. lawyers to assist with the investigation. "It is not necessary for anyone to tell us how to carry out justice. The judge is capable. What we need is collaboration. There is sufficient intelligence in the U.S. to make an analysis of what is occurring. No one remembers anything." (TV 12)

9/26 Congress member Moakley reportedly tells Cristiani that his proposal to invite U.S. jurists "would only muddle the situation." (LPG 9/27)

9/26 Amadeo Artiga, legal specialist, says Cristiani's request for legal assistance from the U.S. is an "unacceptable mistake." "He should first have consulted with legal authorities here. The judge doesn't need advice. He needs cooperation." (TV 12)

9/26 Jesuit Francisco Ibizate of the UCA says Cristiani is "trying to give the appearance of a good judicial system in El Salvador. I would suppose in the U.S. they have the intelligence to see for themselves. It is apparent that military intelligence is better than military memory." (TV 6) Reporter repeats an earlier comment by Ibizate, "If they don't discover anything at the end they will have discovered a lot." (TV 12)

9/27 Eduardo Pineda of the Human Rights Department of the Attorney General's office says the testimony of Colonel Linares yesterday provided "new information," including confirmation that the logistics center for the Atlacatl Battalion was in the Military School. He also confirmed that the commando unit of the Atlacatl was under operational control of the Chief of Staff of the Armed Forces, then of Colonel Benavides. According to Linares, he was not aware of the activities of the commando unit. (Sonora)

9/28 *La Prensa Grafica* publishes portions of the testimony of Colonel Oscar Len Linares on September 26. The Atlacatl Battalion had 1261 troops, three executive officers, fifty-one officers, and nine companies in November, according to Linares. He declared that Colonel Ponce ordered him to send the special forces to San Salvador on the 13th of November, 160 men. The 8th Company was under the command of the High Command, the 7th Company under Linares' command in El Carmen, Ayutuxtepeque, on the north side of the capital.

On November 15 he was informed that the commandos were under the operative command of the Security Command of the Military Complex. "On the night of the 15th I asked Colonel Ponce to return the commando unit to me and he responded he would give them to me as soon as he reorganized the troop displacements. After the meeting I returned to Ayutuxtepeque. At 7:00 am on November 16 the commando unit reincorporated on the north side of the capital on the orders of the High Command and I didn't learn about the assassination of the Jesuits until 10:00 am through a guerrilla radio."

On January 5 General Larios called him to report on ballistics tests which corresponded to one or two weapons of the commando unit. Larios ordered him to disarm the officers and soldiers of the unit and take them to three security forces. In the days prior to the 5th some members were submitted to ballistics tests. One, Alberto Sierra Ascencio deserted when he was on leave.

Linares said he visited his men in the security forces and understood they were under arrest because family members were not allowed to visit. "I left fifteen soldiers in the National Police, two officers and twelve soldiers in the Treasury Police and fourteen soldiers in the National Guard. The majority were returned to me later at the headquarters of the Battalion, Sitio del Niño." He said he did not see Colonel Benavides in the security forces. (LPG)

9/28 *Diario Latino* publishes the entire transcript released to the press. Linares also said his men being held in the National Guard complained they "were located in the same sector where terrorists were being investigated."

According to Linares, while the commando unit was under the command of Benavides it "could not make an operative decision on its own." He confirmed that the Logistics Center of the Atlacatl Battalion was in the Military School and had communications with all units by radio; food, ammunition, extra radios, batteries and uniforms were in the School.

When Lt. Espinoza Guerra reported back to Linares he did not inform him of the operations carried out by the commando unit while it was under orders of the Security Command. A list of names of the men who participated in the raid was turned over to Linares on December 7. (DL)

9/28 "An unprecedented event." Strict security measures as U.S. Major Eric Buckland gives his testimony to Judge Zamora today. The "highly unusual" 8 1/2-hour interview takes place in the home of Ambassador Walker, with defense and prosecution attorneys present; Buckland has two North American attorneys at his side. An attorney for the defense interviewed later says the process, which should have taken 5 hours, was "interrupted repeatedly" by Buckland's attorneys who "repeatedly decided not to answer the questions of the defense." The attorney cites as an example a question as to his relationship with Congress member Moakley. "They said he must not be asked about events after January 6. If he agreed voluntarily to testify he should submit to our laws. Under our law defense attorneys are not allowed to participate in the testimony." (TV 12) Buckland was in El Salvador as a U.S. advisor from October 16-January 6, assigned to C5 of the High Command, under Colonel Carlos Avilés.

9/29   According to a report issued by the Moakley Task Force to Congress on September 14, the Military School log book presented to the Judge "is almost certainly a forgery." The report also mentions that Captain Carlos Herrera Carranza testified that Colonel Mauricio Guzmán Aguilar gave the original orders for the raid on the Jesuit house November 13. The report charges, "a concerted effort has been made by the Armed Forces including the High Command to contain the investigation, to avoid implicating any individual except those charged and almost certainly to prevent the conviction of Colonel Benavides." (NYT 9/25)

9/29   The Rector of the UCA, Miguel Estrada says the investigation is "headed on a legal path that is a dead end. It will not allow us to know who is responsible. The North Americans must force the officers to say what they know because they are the owners of the circus." (Horizonte)

October 1990

10/1 Two Jesuits also testify today; Francisco Javier Ibizate and Tobias Vargas, the legal representative of the UCA, present declarations as to material damages caused to the institution during the night of November 16. Ibizate says, "I didn't want to come. It seems absurd to testify about damages to two vehicles in the context of the massacre. But it helps confirm the material authors." (TV 6) Ibizate declares the questions of the defense attorneys to Major Buckland were "stupid and malicious." "Everyone says, 'I don't remember. I don't remember.' Col. Cerna Flores says he ordered the raid at 8:00 p.m . . . Either he has a very bad memory or it is something else." (TV 12) Ibizate was in the Jesuit house on the night of the raid, but was sleeping in a nearby home on November 16. (Horizonte)

10/1 Prosecuting attorney Sidney Blanco says Major Buckland was "firm and convincing" in his testimony. He was very credible. "The question is who to believe, two colonels or Buckland?" Blanco agrees that the questions of the defense to Buckland about his relationship with Congress member Joe Moakley were "irrelevant." (TV 12) Blanco also says there is no need for a "face-to-face confrontation" between Avilés and Buckland. "Buckland was categoric in stating the day, the hour and the place when he obtained the information of the participation of Colonel Benavides. His words regarding the explanation of what he understood from Colonel Avilés gave more confidence to the prosecution. We have a moral conviction about who we must believe. A confrontation between the two witnesses would be inappropriate. It appears as though the person who has not stated the truth is Colonel Avilés. We noted a certain interest on his part in disavowing the events." Blanco reports that Buckland left the country the same day he testified, September 28. (EM) "Avilés was evasive, concerned about his career and even his life," says Blanco. (DL 10/2)

10/1 President Cristiani meets with President Bush today and assures him he is committed to resolving the Jesuit case. Bush reportedly says, "I want to encourage you to continue what you are trying to do to come to the end of this." (Horizonte) Cristiani asked Bush not to cut aid, noting that any aid cut "benefits the FMLN". "They are planning a new offensive when the aid is reduced." (Sonora)

10/2 According to Major Buckland's testimony, "On the 20th or 21st of December, during conversations in the office of Colonel Avilés, Avilés said he had something important to tell him but it must not be repeated, it was "confidential from Carlos to Eric." Avilés asked him "not to release the information except in case of emergency." He then repeated Benavides' confession to Buckland. Two North American lawyers were with Buckland, John C. Cruden and David Graham. (DH)

10/2 Buckland, 36, was in El Salvador on temporary duty from June 1989 until the end of July 1989. Colonel Avilés requested that he return for permanent duty; the two men were "very friendly" and Avilés called him several times in the States before he returned to El Salvador on October 16, 1989. Buckland said in his testimony that he learned about the assassinations on the afternoon of November 16; because the work of C5 (Department of Psychological Operations) is to "protect the image of the government," he met with Avilés on a daily basis to discuss the case. Buckland is currently assigned to the Special Forces in Fort Bragg. (DL)

10/2 The majority of the 24 officers present at the meeting on November 15 have personally appeared to testify during recent weeks; today Colonel Juan Carlos Carrillo Schlenker of the National Guard sends a notarized statement. Colonel Benjamin Canjura of the CITFA does appear to testify. "He was open and cooperated with us," says the prosecuting attorney. Canjura confirms that operational command of the Armed Forces during the offensive was not the High Command but the COT, Center of Tactical Operations. (TV 6) "This does not mean that the head of COT was responsible for the assassinations." (TV 12) Command of COT was rotated between the Minister of Defense and the Vice-Ministers of Defense and Security, Larios, Zépeda and Montano.

10/3 Colonel Ochóa Pérez says the testimonies of officers in the Jesuit case "contradict each other and create more doubts." He repeats his charge that Colonel Benavides "did not make the decision alone. In all decisions there is a chain of command . . . The contradictions are serious and must be overcome. Someone was responsible, for example someone of the COT (Center for Tactical operations)." (Horizonte)

10/3 Prosecuting attorneys Sidney Blanco and Henry Alfaro Solorzano criticizes the lack of cooperation from the military and SIC. "From the beginning the delegation of the prosecution has been marginalized from SIC information, but information has been passed along to the defense." The two SIC employees who testified this week, Catarino Lovato Ayala and Ismael Parada, "timidly testified that a defense attorney was present during Benavides' declaration to SIC. It is not legal or usual to allow defense attorneys to be present during extrajudicial investigations, at least here . . . It would have been important for the prosecution to have been present. The declaration taken that day does not mention the fact that the defense attorney, Méndez Flores was present. The two witnesses said he requested that his name not be mentioned. This is ridiculous. It is necessary for the people to know how and where this extrajudicial statement occurred and who was present." (EM)

10/4 Pastor Ridreujo, again accompanied by Benjamin Cestoni, visits the courthouse to meet with Judge Zamora; also meets with Supreme Court President Dr. Mauricio Gutierrez Castro and with Foreign Minister Pacas Castro; the latter visit described as a "private meeting." (TV 12)

Dr. Pastor Riereujo after meeting with Judge Zamora tells the press, "It would be the best thing for the country and the Armed Forces to clear this up." (TV 6)

10/4 Prosecuting attorneys in the Jesuit case discuss the progress of the investigation:

"Sergeant Cordoba Monge is the only military witness of the Atlacatl Battalion. He was one of the first to make a declaration and his version stands, contrary to others which are contradictory."

Evidence against Benavides. "The indications are in the testimony of Cordoba Monge, the weapons found in the Military School and the responsibility Benavides had as Commander of the Security Complex.

From there it is difficult to imagine that Benavides did not know what occurred in his area. It is not possible that he did not know. The normal thing is that he would have known."

"There is a report from the Joint Staff in which it says that the Theology Building was damaged at 0:30 hours. At 2:30 a.m. it notes that during an attack the Jesuits were assassinated, that is to say that within the same enemy action. The information is noted and it reveals a previous knowledge of what had happened or was going to happen. It says clearly the "DTs" or "terrorist delinquents," perhaps anticipating preparing the action and the determination that other armed elements, in this case the guerrillas, were responsible."

"The curious thing is that all members of the Armed Forces say they do not know where the report came from."

"Another question that appears noted is that in the morning of the 16th they heard strong explosions coming from the UCA. To give the exact location one must know exactly where it came from."

"However there is secrecy about this; the army says the source was civilian. No one knows."

"Colonel Ponce said in his sworn statement that he had a report from the National Police about a meeting of union members in the UCA but he doesn't say what else he did or what measures were taken. This has been widely criticized in the investigation. It is assumed that the Judge will call Ponce again, not only about this report but about other things that have come up during the investigation and must be clarified . . . It is important that the things be told. It is not possible to leave lies in the air." (DL)

NOTE: Correction: Jesuit Francisco Javier Ibizate was not present in the Jesuit house during the raid on the 13th as reported several days ago. On the night of the massacre he was staying in a home located thirty meters from the UCA. (LPG)

10/5 Colonel Carlos Mauricio Guzmán Aguilar testifies in the Jesuit case today. Guzmán Aguilar was head of the National Police until October 1989, head of DNI (Intelligence) during the offensive and is currently serving as Military Attache to Costa Rica. He says he had "nothing to do with the assassinations. The proof is that if I had been involved I would be in prison." He admits ordering an officer from the DNI to accompany Atlacatl troops during the raid, "in order to know first hand what was there," but says he heard about the assassinations at 8:00 a.m. on the 16th and "no one applauded." (Horizonte)." Some people have tried to relate me or the DNI to the assassinations," he tells the press, "but I had nothing to do with it and I can defend myself." (TV 6) One paper describes the Colonel as "serene" during his testimony. (LPG 10/6)

10/6 The Supreme Court announces approval of President Cristiani's proposal to invite "noted jurists" to review the Jesuit case. (DH)

10/8 Prosecuting attorneys say the Jesuit investigation is at an important point, near the end of interviewing witnesses. A report will be issued next week. (Horizonte)

10/8 "We knew the little ones lied"; says Jesuit José María Tojeira, "now we know the big ones lie too. Our distrust is not hypothetical. Guzmán Aguilar said something very different from Cerna Flores. The conspiracy of silence continues. The officers have followed the example of the President formally but not in spirit; the many contradictions demonstrate there is something else behind it all." (TV 12)

10/8 A detective from the SIC, José Ismael Parada testified that the AK 47 and M60 used in the assassinations of the Jesuits belonged to the Military School; a lieutenant who testified earlier said there were no AKs in the School. (Horizonte)

10/8 President Cristiani says three U.S. jurists will arrive soon to review the investigation. (Horizonte)

10/10 Interviewed on "Buenos Días", María Julia Hérnandez of Tutela Legal charges General Rafael Villamariona of the Air Force of being "as responsible as Colonel Benavides" for the assassinations of the Jesuits and cites a U.S. government document as her source. She also accuses the Embassy of responsibility for the charges of "bias" in the work of Tutela published by the "Washington Inquirer." The article was first distributed in Congress with no attribution, says Hérnandez, and is part of the "covert actions" of the Embassy. (TV 12)

10/10 Hérnandez misinterpreted the document, according to Jesuit Tojeira who tells the press that the heavily censored document only notes Villamariona as a member of the SIC and does not charge him with involvement in the crime. (DL)

10/11 General Villamariona will file legal charges against María Julia Hérnandez. "A person such as she who believes she knows the truth should measure the consequences of her charges. This is serious and tendentious . . . It is part of the systematic work of Tutela Legal to discredit the Armed Forces." (TV 12)

10/11 Hrnandez admits the charges were the result of an error in translation. "He has the right to take me to court. We will decide there. The document only mentions him as the officer of higher rank than any others including Benavides. It was an error in translation, not bad faith. I assume all responsibility." (TV 12)

10/12 According to Colonel Guzmán Aguilar's testimony the DNI had agents located all around the UCA on the night of the 15-16 of November, at the Banco Hipotecario, Ceiba de Guadalupe, Ministry of Foreign Relations, Museo David Guzmán and in the El Chorizo community "but he didn't know anything about the attack." He said that according to intelligence information the FMLN had radio transmitters in La Cima, Lomas de San Francisco, University Albert Einstein, Colonia Theater and in nearby ravines. DNI agent Héctor Ulises Cuenco Ocampo was sent to participate in the raid on the 13th by Captain Fernando Herrera Carranza "in case weapons, propaganda or terrorists were found." (DH) He also said the DNI did not investigate the crime because the SIC had been assigned that responsibility. He participated in the meeting of the High Command on the night of the 15th, then met with Colonel Ivan Diaz and went to his office. (LPG)

10/13 General Villamariona says he was "satisfied" with María Julia Hérnandez's statement but the High Command will decide whether or not to press legal charges. (TV 12)

10/13 President Cristiani is asked by reporters to comment on the fact that Colonel Juan Carlos Schlenker of the National Guard sent a statement to Judge Zamora rather than appear in person as other high ranking officers have during the past weeks. Cristiani says this is a "personal right of military leaders and each one must decide for himself whether or not to use the privilege not to appear. We haven't forced anyone." Judge Zamora says he has begun to issue subpoenas to the remaining officers who have not appeared including Colonel Gilberto Rubio, currently Chief of Staff. (EM)

10/15 Judge Zamora has sent questionnaires to Colonels Ponce, Machuca and Schlenker, to Ponce for the third time. The fundamental question of who was in charge the night of November 15-16 remains unanswered. (TV 12)

10/15 "I am convinced that an act of this nature must have had more intellectual authors," Archbishop Rivera y Damas commented to the press yesterday on the Jesuit case. (EM)

10/16 The United States is not interested in a thorough investigation of the Jesuit case, says UCA Rector Miguel Estrada in Spain, citing the withholding of twenty-one documents on the case by U.S. authorities. According to Estrada, release of the documents "would force them to accept their participation." Estrada also says he is "afraid for the situation of the country...The death squads are still active." (TV 12)

10/17 German Minister of Economic Cooperation, Juergen Warnke says the country has suspended all aid to El Salvador until the Jesuit case is resolved. "Some governments talk about Cristiani's 'good will' but if the investigation to unmask the assassins has not had any results we cannot continue granting development aid to a state which has demonstrated in practice that it cannot punish violations of human rights committed by institutions of the state itself." (DL)

10/17 Prosecuting attorneys in the Jesuit case say if Lt. Col. Manuel Antonio Rivas of the SIC "admits" that Colonel Benavides confessed his responsibility for the crime to Rivas the process will enter the final phase. (EM) Supreme Court President predicts a ruling from Judge Zamora "soon." (DH)

10/18 In reference to the Jesuit investigation, Salvador Samayoa, of the FMLN Political/Diplomatic Commission, states that the possible implication of North Americans "in this and other assassinations, acting on their own or institutionally is a complicated issue which could reveal a different dimension and a probable international connection with the behavior of the Salvadoran Army." (DL/DPA)

10/18 "The U.S. Embassy is blocking the investigation," charges Jesuit Provincial José María Tojeira, citing a report from Congressmember Moakley released today. According to Tojeira, Major Buckland provided information that could "change the case" but the information was not turned over to Judge Zamora. "Some officials of the Embassy have acted in a dirty way," he says, citing, as an example, the treatment of the witness last December. Tojeira also discards President Cristiani's proposal to bring three North American jurists to review the investigation: "There is no need to supervise the Judge . . . It would be better to bring three retired generals to supervise the army." (TV6)

10/19 Lt. José Preza Rivas of SIC testified yesterday but provided no new information, according to the prosecution. (DH)

10/19 "El Salvador wasn't news until they started killing priests," says Jesuit Jon Sobrino in Asturia, Spain. The situation for the Jesuits has been "relatively peaceful" since November, but Sobrino expresses concern that the death squads are still active. (Horizonte)

10/19 The Moakley statement issued yesterday accused the State Department of "hiding important information." Major Buckland apparently told the FBI in February about threats made by a "high level military officer" against the Jesuits days before the massacre but later retracted his statement. U.S. officials "never informed the investigation commission." (Horizonte) The incident involved Colonel Benavides. Moakley said, "I consider this to be an incredible and inexcusable error in judgement." State Department did not respond. (EM)

10/19 Lt. Col. Manuel Antonio Rivas, director of SIC, testifies today from 7:30-11:30 am, and presents a synthesis of the investigation. Rivas says Buckland's testimony was false, that Colonel Benavides never admitted knowledge of the crime to him. He also accuses the witness, Lucia Barrera, of lying. (TV 6) "I would have to have supernatural powers to know what occurred to Buckland for him to say that I received a confession from Benavides." Rivas is the third officer to contradict Major Buckland's testimony, the other two were Colonel Ivan López y López and Colonel Carlos Avilés. (EM 10/20)

10/19 Judge Zamora denies rumors that he received an "important document" from Washington this week (LPG 10/20). Approximately 400 persons have testified to date. (DL)

10/21 After Sunday Mass, Bishop Rosa Chávez comments, "The truth in the Jesuit case is very far away." (TV 12)

10/22 *New York Times* refers to the Senate vote as an "important defeat for the White House . . . motivated by the Jesuit assassinations." (TV 12)